THE GEOGRAPHY OF INSIGHT

THE GEOGRAPHY OF INSIGHT

The Sciences, the Humanities,
How they Differ, Why They Matter

Richard Foley

OXFORD
UNIVERSITY PRESS

OXFORD
UNIVERSITY PRESS

Oxford University Press is a department of the University of Oxford. It furthers
the University's objective of excellence in research, scholarship, and education
by publishing worldwide. Oxford is a registered trade mark of Oxford University
Press in the UK and certain other countries.

Published in the United States of America by Oxford University Press
198 Madison Avenue, New York, NY 10016, United States of America.

CIP data is on file at the Library of Congress
ISBN 978–0–19–086512–2

1 3 5 7 9 8 6 4 2

Printed by Sheridan Books, Inc., United States of America

CONTENTS

CONTENTS

PREFACE

Epistemology is one of the major fields of philosophy. It is the study of what we know and how it is we come to know it. Most of my scholarly work has been in epistemology, but a second part of my professional life has been university administration. I was Dean of the Faculty of Arts and Science at New York University for almost a decade. Previously I had been Dean of Arts and Science at Rutgers University and Chair of its Department of Philosophy, and prior to that Chair of the Department of Philosophy at the University of Notre Dame.

The Arts and Science schools at NYU and Rutgers span the humanities (Art History, English, History, Music, Philosophy, etc.), the social sciences (Anthropology, Economics, Politics, Sociology, etc.), and the sciences (Biology, Chemistry, Computer Science, Mathematics, Neuroscience, Physics, Psychology, etc.). In other words, pretty much every discipline that is not a part of a professional school is within Arts and Science.

Among the most interesting responsibilities of deans are those involved with hiring and promoting faculty. Each hire and promotion involves an elaborate review process that includes a departmental recommendation to the dean. The recommendation is not just a simple "yes" or "no" but a detailed review by the faculty in the department of the candidate's scholarship and teaching. To aid it in its deliberation, the department solicits confidential letters from experts in the candidate's field at other universities, which assess the quality and impact of the candidate's research. All this material is sent to the dean's office, where further letters from outside specialists are obtained. The entire packet of materials (the departmental assessments of teaching and research, the letters from the department's evaluators, and the letters from the dean's evaluators) is then reviewed by the dean's promotion and tenure committee, which is made up of senior scholars across a range of disciplines. This committee provides advice to the dean about whether to approve the recommendation of the department.

At Rutgers, there are separate promotion and tenure committees for candidates in the humanities, social sciences, and sciences, whereas at NYU there is a single committee consisting of senior faculty drawn from the full range of arts and science departments, the rationale being that this helps ensure that university-wide standards are met. Physicists and economists examine the credentials of historians; literature scholars and political scientists assess chemists; and biologists and philosophers judge sociologists.

In eighteen years as dean at NYU and Rutgers, I attended more than seven hundred meetings of promotion and tenure committees at which the scholarship and teaching of candidates from the humanities, social sciences, and sciences were assessed. This is a rich set of data for observing similarities and differences across academic fields.

I began taking notes on these similarities and differences while I was dean at Rutgers and the pace of note taking increased at

NYU. When I stepped down from administration, I decided to take a stab at putting eighteen years of scattered notes into a coherent form. The result is this book, which examines the epistemologies of the humanities and sciences: the kinds of insights, knowledge, and understanding that each produces when all goes well. And frequently enough, things do go well.

People are impressed by different things. Toward the top of my list are intellectual achievements that are products of years and sometimes even decades of work. One of the nicest aspects of being a dean—there are less pleasant ones as well—is that one comes across numerous examples of such achievements. I mention this because I have a polemical as well as explanatory aim here. In an era attached to sound bites and tweets and immediately useful results, this essay is intended to be a defense of a culture of research. Such a culture has many facets, but above all else it is one that treasures and finds ways to support long-term intellectual achievements. Its presiding value is that with respect to many issues it ought not to be easy to have opinions.

One of the main responsibilities of universities is that of creating and sustaining a culture of research. Other institutions, such as libraries, centers of advanced study, and academic societies, also have a responsibility to support research, but for universities the ties to research are both profound and bound up with their histories.

The structures and missions of contemporary research universities have been heavily influenced by European universities of the eighteenth and nineteenth centuries, but universities and other centers of advanced learning have a much longer history and one that is distributed across all regions of the world. Among the earliest and most celebrated were the schools of ancient Greece, Plato's Academy and its various offshoots, including Aristotle's Lyceum, which anticipated contemporary universities by systematically collecting knowledge across a variety of subjects, from the scientific to the historical, cultural, and political. Egypt had its legendary library at Alexandria, which for three centuries, from its founding in the third century B.C.E. to the Roman conquest of Egypt, attracted scholars across Africa, Europe, and Asia for the study of mathematics, languages, and philosophy. In China, centers of learning date from even earlier times, but it was the Imperial Central Academy at Nanjing, founded in the third century C.E., that is usually regarded as its first comprehensive institution of research. In India and Japan, Buddhist monasteries focused on Buddhist studies but also trained students in medicine, mathematics, astronomy, politics, and fine arts. Other religions in other regions of the world established analogous centers. The mosques of Timbuktu, in what is now Mali, had Islamic subjects as their primary concern, but they too attracted scholars across a wide range of fields: medicine, astronomy, mathematics, physics, chemistry, philosophy, languages, and geography.

There are many other examples as well, but it was in Europe in the medieval period when the number of institutions dedicated to advanced studies increased dramatically, with monks and priests moving out of monasteries and into cities to establish schools. During this period, universities were founded at Bologna, Paris, Oxford, Cambridge, and many other cities. It was not until the eighteenth and nineteenth centuries, however, that these institutions began to resemble contemporary research universities, with the German model being especially influential in large part because it was research oriented.

Institutions of higher learning have played indispensable roles over the centuries in the collection, preservation, and production of knowledge. Where and when individual institutions have flourished has varied. Sometimes in this place, other times in that place, and once established they haven't always survived. Many eventually became victims of political, religious, or economic change, but when they perished or weakened in one region, centers elsewhere helped limit the damage.

In the twentieth century, it had sometimes seemed that the battles to preserve, produce, and value knowledge were largely over, with the exception of a few skirmishes over this or that issue and a few regions of the world here and there. Now, from a vantage point well into the twenty-first century, it is easy and painful to see this is not the case. And so it is that just as universities, as one of the most long-lived of human institutions, have been critical in other epochs, in our time they again have a special role to play in nurturing scholarship and valuing learning.

This being said, it has become increasingly challenging for them to do so. Political and cultural forces have eroded respect for specialized knowledge and expertise,[1] helped along by the accusation that disinterested inquiry and opinion are myths, left over illusions from simpler times. A modest and healthy reaction to this accusation is concessionary: "Human inquirers are imperfect. So yes, perfect neutrality is not in the offing, but disinterestedness can still function as an ideal that inquirers can do better or worse jobs at approximating even if they never fully realize it."

Unfortunately, wherever there is imperfection, there are also purist impulses to write off whatever is not spotless. These impulses may be a mark of immaturity, but they are no less prevalent for being such. With respect to the intellectual issues, they can easily provide an excuse for quick dismissals of conclusions one does not like. For if the ways inquirers deal with issues are inevitably less than wholly disinterested, one may feel entitled to write off results that are in tension with one's own political or pragmatic interests. One need

1. Tom Nichols, *The Death of Expertise* (New York: Oxford University Press, 2017).

not intellectually engage the arguments. Since the conclusions are inacceptable, so too must be the considerations that led to them.

Once one has started down this slippery slope, it is hard to stop. It is but a small additional step to adopt the same attitude toward information itself. It too gets evaluated in political and practical terms, with the inconvenient being discounted and the favorable being highlighted. Ditto for the notion of expertise. One expert is as good as another. You have yours. I have mine.

The politicization of expertise and information has been accompanied by, and often enough contributed to, an undermining of financial support for research and higher education generally. It is more accurate to say, however, that this is so in some regions of the world but not all. One of the peculiarities of our time is that many countries with little in the way of research infrastructure or traditions of higher education are now eagerly building them, while the countries that have been the envy of the rest of the world for their universities and research capacities seem to be losing their appetite for maintaining them.

Following my years as dean, I spent several additional years in administration working with NYU's newly established degree-granting campuses in Abu Dhabi and Shanghai. These campuses are a major component of each country's long-term plan to invest aggressively in higher education and research. In China, the hope is to reverse the damage done by the Cultural Revolution, when universities across the country were closed and scholars dismissed from their positions. The United Arab Emirates is a much newer country, founded only in 1971, and it sees sustained support for advanced learning as one of the key factors in its project of nation building.

In the United States, the cultural moment is much different, with at best wavering support for higher education and research, and with what support there is increasingly tilted toward short-term goals. State research universities have been especially hard hit, with the effects of an uncertain funding environment for research being magnified by large decreases in the percentage of their budgets supported by the states. The current atmosphere stands in contrast to the decades following World War II, which produced a golden period of higher education and research in the United States. So successful were the investments during this period that US universities came to dominate the international rankings of universities. The Academic Ranking of World Universities, often called the "Shanghai Ranking," assesses universities solely on the basis of their research profiles. Its 2017 ranking has eight US universities in its list of the ten best research universities of the world, and as one goes further down the list, there are sixteen US institutions in the list of the top twenty, and twenty-nine in the list of the top fifty. The 2018 *London Times* Higher Education Ranking, in which research is one of several criteria, reaches similar results: seven of its top eleven universities (there is a tie for tenth), fifteen of its top twenty, and twenty-six of the top fifty are US based.

If one adds in the rankings of universities in the United Kingdom, the picture that emerges is even more striking. In the Shanghai Ranking, all ten of its top ten research universities are located either in the United States or the United Kingdom. Of the top twenty, nineteen are in the United States or United Kingdom, and of the top fifty, the number is thirty-six . In the *Times* Ranking, the results again are similar: ten out of the top eleven are US or UK based; nineteen of the top twenty, and thirty-three of the top fifty. And yet, in the United Kingdom as in the United States, support for higher education in recent years has been tepid.

If the United States and United Kingdom "decide," if only by inaction or political stalemate, that their time at the apex of higher education has ended, other countries will gladly take their place, thereby attracting a greater share of the top international schol-ars, the best students, and the most important research projects. Supporting research and higher education need not be a zero-sum game, however. A continuation of the tradition of strong research cultures in the United States and United Kingdom is compatible with there being flourishing research cultures and universities in other parts of the world. There is no scarcity of important projects waiting to be done and no foreseeable end to the need for uni-versities to train new generations to students capable of working on them.

There are, however, two commitments that have been at the core of universities throughout their history and remain critical today for building and preserving robust research traditions. The first is a commitment to a long view and its attendant recognition that not every inquiry is to be assessed in terms of its short-term usefulness. Long gestation periods are often needed.[2] The second is a com-mitment to a broad view, with an appreciation for the full breadth of issues of interest to humans. The two reinforce one another. Important insights in one area often have long-term, unforeseen implications in seemingly far removed fields. The history of com-puting is an object lesson in the potential synergies between the long and the broad, with work in the late nineteenth and early twen-tieth centuries by mathematicians and philosophers on two-valued logics being utilized a century later by computer scientists to create electronic circuits of immense power.[3]

2. A classic defense of the long view can be found in Abraham Flexner's 1939 essay, "The Usefulness of Useless Knowledge." Flexner's essay along with a companion piece by Robbert Dijkgraaf, "The World of Tomorrow," can be found in A. Flexner, *The Usefulness of Useless Knowledge* (Princeton, NJ: Princeton University Press, 2017).

3. For an approachable retelling of this history, see Chris Dixon, "How Aristotle Created the Computer," *The Atlantic*, March 20, 2017. Other examples of these synergies can be found in Flexner's and Dijkgraaf's essays, in Flexner, *Usefulness of Useless Knowledge*.

Neither long views nor broad views are in abundant supply in our time, which makes it all the more important for universities to cherish and support long-term intellectual endeavors across a range of fields. Sometimes the humanities and sciences are thought of as being in competition with one another, but with respect to this issue they are fellow travelers. A healthy culture for research for both is necessary for either to thrive in the long run.

But if universities are to nourish both the sciences and the humanities, they need to understand them. My central claim in this work is that this involves appreciating that the intellectual aims of the two tend to be different, and this is not to be regretted. On the contrary, it is a good thing. A very good thing. Their differences complement one another.

R.F.

THE GEOGRAPHY OF INSIGHT

Chapter 1

The Humanities
and Sciences Are Different

Put the basic sciences into one group: physics, chemistry, biology, mathematics. Then the humanities in another. My question is whether inquiries in the two groups should have different intellectual aims. By this I mean the kinds of insights that ought to be expected from them. Here are two closely related questions: Are the values informing inquiries in the sciences typically different from those in the humanities, and should they be?

I think the answer to all these questions is "yes." I will be arguing that there are four major differences:

1. The sciences value findings that are not limited to particular locations, times, or things. The ideal is to arrive at generalizations that are accurate for everything, every time, and every location, or if this proves too difficult, with as few exceptions as possible. In the humanities, such generalizations are not so valued, nor should they be. Its concerns are more limited in scope. They are ones about humans and their societies, and usually not even about all humans or all human societies. They are instead about particular people (or groups of them)

at particular locations and times. In dealing with such issues, to exert pressure for greater and greater generalization at best risks glossing over important details. At worst, it is an invitation to shallowness. An indexical term, to make use of a notion from linguistics, is one that makes reference to a specific time, location, person, or thing. So, a shorthand way of expressing this difference between the sciences and the humanities is to say that the sciences value results that are minimally indexical, whereas in the humanities reducing indexicality to a minimum need not be so valued and usually isn't.

2. The sciences treasure findings that are as independent as possible of the perspectives of those conducting the inquiry. Minimizing the influence of perspective reduces the risk of distortion and also broadens the potential audience. It increases the prospects of the results being intelligible to those with different perspectives, perhaps even to sufficiently intelligent creatures with perceptual and cognitive faculties different from humans, if there are such beings somewhere in the universe. This is not and should not be the aim in the humanities. Their issues require an understanding of the conscious states and points of view of humans. Human inquirers have a built-in advantage with respect to these issues. They have knowledge of what human consciousness is like from their own case, and it is appropriate for them to make use of this knowledge in treatments of their issues as opposed to trying to leave as few traces of their perspectives as possible. But to the extent that the conclusions reached reflect the inquirer's perspective, it becomes less likely that they will be intelligible to those whose locations, histories, faculties, and hence perspectives are quite different. The audience is thus a more restricted one, and the inquiries themselves have to

be conducted with the intended audiences and their perspectives in mind.

3. The aim of the sciences is to be descriptive. Inquirers are expected to limit themselves to describing and explaining what is (or was or will be) the case, whereas this need not be the sole aim in the humanities. Their issues are often concerned with prescriptive claims as well as descriptive ones. Prescriptive claims give expression to values. They make recommendations about what should be (or should have been) the case. Thus, to cite but one example, it is not at all out of place for historical accounts of the Battle of Waterloo not only to describe the details of the battle but also assess whether there were decisions that Napoleon should have made differently.

4. The sciences are organized around the importance of increasing the stock of collective knowledge. The individual insights that are most prized are those that contribute to what is collectively agreed upon and known. In the humanities, individual insight is highly valued for its own sake, independently of its ability to generate consensus. Indeed, many of the issues are such that it is not feasible to expect agreement, not even in the long run.

None of these distinctions is all-or-nothing. Each is a matter of degree. The thesis here is thus to be understood as one about the relative emphases, default values, and pressures in the two domains. There is, moreover, enormous variety in both the sciences and humanities. So, blanket generalizations about everything that goes in either area are not to be expected. What links the various sciences are their family resemblances with one another. They are connected through a series of overlapping similarities, and the same is true of the humanities. In what follows, I will be discussing examples of the variety one finds within each of the two domains, but the primary focus will be on the differences in their reigning paradigms. In inquiries regarded as exemplars of basic science, there is an emphasis on minimizing indexical, perspectival, and prescriptive elements, and on increasing collective knowledge, whereas inquiries most representative of the humanities tend to value knowledge that is highly indexical, perspectival, prescriptive, and individual.

In everyday contexts, terms such as "knowledge," "understanding," and "insight" are used loosely and for the most part interchangeably, and I too will be using them as such. It might be possible to develop clear-cut distinctions among them, but these would be more in the form of recommendations for improving everyday language rather than reports on it. Besides, for my purposes, following the ordinary loose usage creates a big tent and as such helps to avoid getting bogged down in terminological disputes. For example, if along the way a complaint arises that contrary to what I suggest, it is not possible, in the strictest philosophical sense of the term, to have knowledge of the matter in question, I will shrug and say, "So be it; as long there can be understanding or insights about it, that is good enough."

The arts fit into this essay in a special way. I will be more concerned with how the humanities treat works of art than the works themselves, but on the occasions when I do directly discuss them, my focus will be upon the kinds of insights they are capable of producing. Not because this is the sole matter of importance in thinking about the arts, but because it is what's relevant for this essay. It is relevant in a specific way, moreover. The insights the arts are best suited to produce are individual, perspectival, indexical, and prescriptive, the very kinds that are also most characteristic of the humanities, this being one source of the deep links between them.

The social sciences occupy a position between the sciences and the humanities. This is only a rough generalization, however. When one looks at the social sciences, one sees enormous diversity, with some inquiries closely resembling the natural sciences, others the humanities, and yet others somewhere in-between. I return briefly to the social sciences in chapter 4 ("Related Topics"), but until then I will be setting them to one side in order to make the case that the aims of the humanities and science typically are and ought to be different.

The contrary view is that they are fundamentally alike, with identical aims and values. If one ascends to high enough levels of generalization, one can always find resemblances. A field of beans and one of wild flowers look pretty much the same from an altitude of 35,000 feet. So too the best inquiries in both the sciences and the humanities are driven by deep curiosity, an openness to being puzzled, and a determination not to be satisfied with superficial answers. When one descends from the heights, however, one begins to see differences. The differences, I have already said, come in degrees and are best thought of in terms of relative emphases and paradigmatic values, but they are no less the important for being such.

Advocates of the humanities are sometimes uneasy about acknowledging such differences, the fear being that given the prestige of the sciences, the humanities will be judged inferior. But this is a misplaced impulse. It produces the opposite of the desired result. If the sciences and the humanities were alike, the criteria for success would also be alike, but then it inevitably will seem as if the humanities do not measure up. A compelling defense of the humanities is possible only once it is recognized that their aims and values ought to be different from those of the sciences.

The thesis that the aims of the humanities and sciences differ is hardly original. The hermeneutic tradition has especially made a point of distinguishing the natural sciences from the "human sciences," where the latter is meant to include not only the humanities but also the social sciences and law. The basic contrast is said to be that the natural sciences search for explanations, while in the human sciences the search is for understanding.[1] There are also many outside the hermeneutic tradition who have made analogous claims.

The views I will be defending thus have numerous overlaps with those made by others, but I will be exploring fresh ways of making them. Fresh not so much because the features I use to distinguish the sciences and humanities are especially unusual. On the contrary, they are relatively familiar ones, but this has the advantage, I hope, of producing clarity without the need for a lot of controversial theoretical baggage.

What is new is the way I will be marshaling these features to mark off the proper intellectual aims of the humanities from those of the sciences. New too are the links between these features and a set of secondary distinctions between the humanities and the sciences: different attitudes about the possibility of there being an endpoint of inquiry; different notions of intellectual progress; different roles for intellectual expertise; different working assumptions about simplicity and complexity; and different degrees of involvement and comfort with what I shall be calling "mentality."

These primary and secondary characteristics can be thought of as defining the intellectual geography of the humanities and sciences. They map the kinds of insights one can expect to find in the two domains.

1. See, e.g., Wilhelm Dilthey, *The Formation of the Historical World in the Human Sciences*, ed. R. Makkreel and F. Rodi (Princeton, NJ: Princeton University Press, 2002).

Chapter 2

The Distinctions

INDEXICAL VS. NON-INDEXICAL

Indexical claims are localized. They are about particular times, places, or things. Non-indexical claims have no restrictions. They are intended to be universal. They are about all times, places, and things without exception. Like the other distinctions, this one comes in degrees. Such terms as "now," "here," "you," "I," "we," "this," and "that" are all sure signs of high degrees of indexicality. The same is true for claims with proper names (Christopher Columbus, the Eiffel Tower, the Galapagos Islands, etc.) or specific dates (Bastille Day, 9/11, etc.). The more localized the claim, that is, the more specific the times, places, and locations being referred to, the more highly indexical it is. At the other end of the spectrum, the fewer the exceptions, that is, the fewer the times, places, and things that are excluded, the less indexical the claim is.

Conclusions that are highly indexical are often just what are sought in the humanities, whereas in the sciences, especially the basic sciences, there is pressure to arrive at results that are as non-indexical as possible. The paradigmatic issues of the sciences concern the fundamental processes and forces governing physical objects, from the very large (galaxies, planets, oceans, etc.), to the very small (molecules, atoms, quarks, etc.) and those governing living organisms (microbes, plant species, animal species, etc.). The search is for minimally indexical understanding of these processes and forces.

Consider the modern theory of gravitation, which can be traced to the experiments of Galileo that in turn led to Newton's monumental work. It attempts to describe the attraction objects with mass have for one another not only on Earth, and not only in our Milky Way galaxy, and not only over the last thousand years or even million years, but rather for all times, places, and things. The aim is to remove all traces of indexicality.

This has turned out to be a frustratingly difficult goal to achieve. For a couple of hundred years or so, Newton's laws of gravitation were regarded as universal, but increasingly precise astronomical observations eventually surfaced problems. Einstein's general theory of relativity corrected the shortcomings, but he and others soon realized that the new theory seemed incompatible with quantum mechanics. So, it too had restricted applicability. The search for a universal theory of gravitation continues to this day.

The details of this search matter less than the values animating it. Unimaginably small and inconceivably large objects make up the universe, seemingly with idiosyncratic properties. As a result, the quest for a theory of gravity that applies to everything at every time and place is exceedingly complicated. Still, this is the ideal, and it remains such even if there are limitations on fully meeting it. As with other ideals that cannot be completely realized, the ambition is to approach it as closely as possible, which means reducing to a minimum the times, places, and things to which the theory does not apply. When faced with exceptions, the rule is to keep looking and pushing in the direction of ever less indexicality.

But not all science is physics. Consider geology and its theory of plate tectonics, which explains large-scale motions on Earth's surface, such as earthquakes, volcanic activity, mountain building, and ocean trench formation. Earth is but one planet in a large universe, and it is a planet that has existed for a relatively brief period of astronomical time. The best current estimate of its age is 4.5 billion years, which is only one-third of the estimated age of the universe.

The insights being sought are thus indexical, which geologists provide by describing a set of standing conditions and forces operating on them. The standing conditions are ones about the different layers of the planet and their distinct properties, most important, the lithosphere, which is the mostly rigid top layer consisting of separate plates, and the layer beneath it, the asthenosphere, which flows in a liquid-like way over geological time periods. The key finding is that the plates of the lithosphere float on the more fluid-like asthenosphere, with a set of physical forces determining their movements over time. The forces are the familiar ones of heat conduction, heat convection, friction, and gravitation.

The forces, in other words, are ones whose applications are not limited to Earth or the times of its existence. They are universal or at least nearly so, and the ways in which they operate upon the standing conditions need not be peculiar to Earth. Other planets at other times in other regions of the universe with similar standing conditions would exhibit similar surface movements. So, although knowledge here is indexical, it is derived from more basic knowledge that isn't.

The same pattern is found elsewhere. Evolutionary biology is concerned with the evolutionary histories of life forms on Earth. This too is indexical knowledge, which again is provided by identifying a set of standing conditions and universal or almost universal processes operating on them. The standing conditions are the phenotypes, genotypes, and environments of living organisms, and the processes are those of natural selection and genetic drift. Efforts to understand how there initially came to be any living organisms at all on Earth are less far along, but the aim is similar. It is to identify the processes that turned lifeless chemical matter present on early Earth into the first simple, living cells, processes that would be capable of doing so elsewhere in the universe were the circumstances similar.[1]

But just as not all science is physics, there are sciences that do not resemble physics but do not resemble biology or geology either. Some do not seek to explain at all. Their primary aim is to survey, describe, and catalog. The taxonomy of orchids provides detailed descriptions of the leaves, stems, roots, flowers, fruits, and seeds of the various orchid species on Earth and organizes important differences into a classificatory system. Because decisions about what constitutes an important difference can reflect different theoretical stances, taxonomies can have explanatory elements.[2] Still, the goal of explaining takes a back seat to that of surveying and describing. As such, taxonomies and other projects of surveying and cataloging are not regarded as examples of fundamental science even if they are of undeniable value. It is also not a coincidence that amateurs can make important contributions to these projects. Think of the Audubon Society Christmas Bird Count, the Citizen Sky Project, and the Monarch Larva Monitoring Project.

There are many other kinds of scientific inquiries that also produce highly indexical knowledge, for example, those concerned with the lives, social arrangements, habitats, and life cycles of animals

---

1. For example, see the website of Harvard's Origin of Life Initiative, http://origins.harvard.edu.
2. Stephen Jay Gould, *Wonderful Life* (New York: W. W. Norton, 1990).

on Earth. These projects, often called "natural histories" (a term that suggests affinities with the kinds of knowledge sought in the humanities), investigate such questions as: How long do individuals of the species in question live on average? What are their typical habitats? What is their diet? What are their social groupings? How do they reproduce? These investigations are again not regarded as paradigms of basic science. The knowledge being sought, although appealing and valuable, is too decidedly indexical. It concerns the lives and life cycles of specific creatures living in particular places and at particular times.

Or consider viticulture. The knowledge base that experienced vintners draw upon is often the product of long histories of trial and error, and not infrequently passed down orally from one generation to another. Much of the knowledge is also robustly indexical, being of the form that vines of a specific type do well in this location but not so well in that location. Still, in such fields there is pressure, especially among those whose livelihoods depend on it, to make the knowledge more general. The working assumption is that underneath the local knowledge, there are specifiable factors, having to do with climate, terrain, and soil, that account for when and where vines of a certain kind tend to do well. To the extent that these factors can be codified, it may be possible to predict yields more accurately and hence reduce risks. It is not surprising, therefore, that there are now many training programs and schools of viticulture and oenology.

Even this handful of examples gives a sense of the variety one finds across the sciences when it comes to indexicality, but there are a couple of general takeaways. First, the greater the emphasis there is in a field on applications, as is the case in agricultural science and pretty much any engineering field, the less pressure there will be on reducing indexicality to a minimum. Second, if the sciences were to be ranked on an indexicality scale, at the end where minimizing it is most valued, one finds fields that are regarded as paradigms of basic science, whereas at the other end are fields that are not regarded as such.

There is no comparable emphasis on reducing indexicality throughout most of the humanities. Think about the numerous studies that have been done on the influence of modernism on European and American architecture, art, and literature in the late nineteenth and early twentieth centuries. These investigations unabashedly are seeking insights about a particular time and region of the world, and there are not the pressures one finds in the sciences to show how the insights can be derived from more basic knowledge that is non-indexical. So too it is with other projects in the humanities, whether they are about the causes and effects of the Hundred Years War between England and France, the characteristics of Athenian democracy, or the features and significance of the Harlem Renaissance. The insights sought are highly indexical—ones about particular times, events, people, societies, and practices.

What degree of indexicality is best suited to produce the desired insights is always a legitimate question, however. Among historians, there are those who in the search for understanding focus on a few especially prominent individuals and events. Others go down a level and concentrate more on the details of ordinary people in their everyday lives. Still others go up a level and direct their attention to motivating political ideas or underlying economic pressures. Some go up yet further and treat the issues under study as the effects of a larger, more long-term system, one in whose workings individual and collective agency are not so central. Think of accounts that attempt to explain the differential paces of societal transformations in different regions of the world in terms of such factors as climate differences and diversity of plant and animal species as opposed to social or political factors.[3]

Historians pick the dimension they think is most important to fix upon in order to make the past intelligible, where importance, as always, is a function of context and purpose, including the value of doing history in general. As a result, there is no agreed-upon, single best way of providing historical understanding, but this is as it should be. In the search for historical understanding, there is always room for questions of how far back to go, where to look, and how widely or narrowly to look.[4]

In addition, even after these questions are settled, it is not the case that the only insights of interest are those about the particular events or contexts that are the immediate objects of study. Works in the humanities can escape their primary subject matters to reveal structures, patterns, and dependencies that can lead to insights elsewhere. Histories of past societies can have parallels with our own recent history; analyses of contemporary literary trends may make clearer the significance of earlier works; and portrayals of a cultural practice in one society can surface features relevant for understanding analogous practices in other societies.

There are limits, however. There are general insights to be had in the humanities, but they do not have the form of hard-and-fast generalizations that can be used to make predictions or deduce explanations about other times, places, and situations. Nor should the goal be to arrive at generalizations as close to this as possible. The insights

3. See Jared Diamond, *Guns, Germs, and Steel: The Fates of Human Societies* (New York: W. W. Norton, 1997); and Peter Burke, *The French Historical Revolution: The Annales School, 1929-2014*, 2nd ed. (Palo Alto, CA: Stanford University Press, 2015).
4. Daniel Little, "Philosophy of History," in *The Stanford Encyclopedia of Philosophy* (Winter 2012 ed.), ed. Edward N. Zalta, http://plato.stanford.edu/archives/win2012/entries/history/.

are instead ones that can be instructive in a this-is-often-the-case kind of way when thinking about other situations. And even here, there are limitations on how wide the scope can be. The more dissimilar the contexts are from one another, the less likely it is that insights about the one will be helpful in understanding the other. It is sometimes remarked that a mark of genuinely great works in the humanities is that their insights are universal, but this is an exaggeration. Even the most perceptive accounts of the social and political conditions in France at the time of French Revolution are unlikely to produce insights that will be of substantial help in understanding early Inuit societies.

The humanities are closely aligned with the arts, and it is similarly not unusual to single out great works of art by saying that their themes are universal. Shakespeare's plays are commonly so praised, but once again for all the splendor of his best work, neither *Hamlet* nor *Richard III* nor *Twelfth Night* is going to be of much relevance for understanding the lives of the early humans in Europe of 40,000 to 10,000 years ago. Nor should they be. From what can be inferred from the remains of huts, cave paintings, carvings, and weapons of these early humans, their social groups lacked many of the characteristics of human societies of the last several thousand years. They have little in common with Shakespeare's portrayals of Hamlet's Denmark, Richard III's England, or Viola's Illyria.

Besides, even if it somehow could be argued that the finest works in the humanities and arts were relevant to understanding the lives and societies of all modern humans, even the earliest, this would still be indexical knowledge. It is knowledge about particular creatures (modern humans) that exist at a particular place (Earth) and a particular time (roughly, the last two hundred thousand years).

Here is a humility producing exercise described by John McPhee. Stretch your arms as widely as you are able. Now think of the distance between the outstretched fingertips of the two hands as a time line that represents the entire history of the Earth. The period of multicellular life forms on Earth is represented by only one of your hands, and the period of human life by only the thickness of a single fingernail.[5]

Knowledge about a brief stretch of time on a single small planet in a very large universe is universal only on a preposterously human-centric view of time and place. Universal by local standards, as it were. Once one takes a step back from the cliché that it is the "time-less" and "universal" that is sought in the humanities and looks in detail at successful instances of humanities research, one finds that most do not even aspire to be free of indexicality. The aim, rather, is to understand something about an indexical "us" or "them," an indexical "here" or "there," or an indexical "now" or "then." This is just what is to be expected, given that the issues of greatest concern to the humanities arise within the limited subset of times and places associated with modern human societies.

What are some of these issues? There are too many to list, but the following are representative: How did various societies, cultural practices, political systems, religions, and intellectual assumptions come into being and how have they changed over time? What are the important commonalities and differences among them? How have economic, social, political, geographical, and other such factors shaped their development and were these influences for better or worse? How have specific individuals or groups contributed to their features, what was it about them or their situations that allowed them to have this influence, and was their influence positive, negative, or a mixture of the two? What roles have works of literature, music, art, and other cultural products played in individual

5. John McPhee, *Basin and Range* (New York: Farrar, Straus and Giroux, 1980), 126.

lives and human societies, how have the attributes of these works differed over time and place, what accounts for these differences, and what are successful and unsuccessful examples of such works? What is the nature of morality and justice, what concrete claims are they thought to make on us, and how have different societies and times interpreted these claims? What are the responsibilities that individuals have to themselves, their families, their governments, strangers, future generations, and the various other groups with which they are associated (their religion, ethnic group, neighborhood, place of work), and what are their responsibilities to other living things?

Information about the characteristic features of humans, including their biological and genetic make-up, can be relevant in addressing many of these issues. So, there is a role for the sciences to play in inquiries about them. It just cannot be the lead. Because the issues are so contextually situated, insights about them have to be likewise steeped in information, concepts, and values associated with particular times, places, and societies—highly indexical considerations, in other words.

Thus, to adapt an example from Bernard Williams, although science may someday help us to better understand why humans everywhere make and enjoy music, it is not going to be of much use in understanding the place of Mozart's operas within the history of opera and the society of eighteenth-century Europe. Here what is of most interest is richly detailed indexical knowledge.[6]

I will have more to say about these differences between the sciences and the humanities in the section titled "Simplicity and Complexity," and in a later section on philosophy I discuss how that

6. Bernard Williams, *Essays and Reviews, 1959-2002* (Princeton, NJ: Princeton University Press, 2014), 412.

discipline tends to place a greater emphasis on reducing indexicality than the rest of the humanities.

PERSPECTIVAL VS. NON-PERSPECTIVAL

"This is how things *now* look to *me* from *here*" is an epitome of both perspectivality and indexicality. The two are interwoven. Efforts to minimize the one create pressure to minimize the other, this being the default dynamic of the sciences. In the humanities, the dynamic is reversed. The need for perspectival insights reinforces the need for indexical insights, and vice versa.

The notion of a perspective, along with its sibling notion of a point of view, has a cluster of meanings, but they all revolve around indexical features of inquirers and their contexts. Inquirers have specific perceptual faculties and cognitive abilities; they occupy particular positions in space-time; they live in distinctive physical and social environments; and within these environments, they have their own peculiar histories, experiences, and memories.

These factors link inquirers to the world and influence the background information they have, the concepts and categories they employ, and the values they adhere to, all of which in turn shape the ways they conduct their inquiries and the conclusions reached. Moreover, all these elements are contingent. They would have been different had the inquirers possessed different faculties and abilities, occupied different physical or social environments, or had different histories and experiences within their environments. It can be an appropriate goal of inquiry, however, to seek insights that are as independent as possible of perspectival factors. Projects in the sciences tend to fall into this category.

The emphasis on diminishing the influence of the inquirer's perspective is on display in pretty much all the core practices of the sciences: the requirement that experiments be replicable; the insistence on publicly observable and quantifiable results; the use of instruments to measure the quantities; the tradition of team conducted research; the importance of collective knowledge; the associated emphasis on findings that can be readily transferred from one investigator to another; and the reliance on mathematics as the language of science. These staples of scientific research are intended to reduce the risks of distortions that can arise from the idiosyncrasies of an inquirer's perspective, but they also broaden the potential audience. They do so by encouraging the development of theories that are not tightly bound to the location, experiences, and history of any single inquirer or a group of them.

A familiar refrain of the sciences is that the structure of things can be quite different from how they appear. Accordingly, it is important not to be overly dependent on initial perceptions. The development of astronomy over the centuries from geocentric views to heliocentric views is an example of how deceiving the surface appearances of phenomena can be to human observers and how science can work to overcome this limitation. Another example is current physics, which posits a world of subatomic particles, fields, and probability waves that are colorless, tasteless, and odorless. This "scientific image" of the world is a far cry from the "manifest image" of three-dimensional objects that humans experience as having colors, tastes, odors, and textures.[7]

---

7. The expressions "scientific image" and "manifest image" are from Wilfrid Sellars, *Science, Perception and Reality* (London: Routledge & Kegan Paul, 1963); reissued in 1991 by Ridgeview Publishing Co., Atascadero, CA.

The theories making up the scientific image are largely expressed with mathematical models. This too is not an accident. Natural languages can be imprecise, and because they evolved in specific contexts for particular purposes, they are repositories of indexical and perspectival information. This is part of their charm and among the reasons they are important for the humanities, but it is also why that they are often not as well suited for the sciences, where the goal is to develop insights as non-indexical and non-perspectival as possible, and potentially understandable by as wide a range as possible of other sufficiently advanced inquirers.

The phrase "sufficiently advanced" is deliberately capacious. It is meant to allow for the possibility of the insights being understood not only by human inquirers in a wide variety of circumstances, provided they have the requisite intelligence, training, and background information, but conceivably even by intelligent creatures who have different perceptual and cognitive faculties from humans and thus experience the world quite differently. In the pursuit of generalizations that are universal or nearly so, the working assumption of the sciences is not that such truths are accessible only to those whose perspectives happen to be similar to those conducting the inquiry—exactly the reverse. The presupposition is that the best way to pursue such generalizations is to escape to the degree possible the locally conditioned contingencies that have shaped one's own perspective.

For human inquirers, these contingencies include short lives on a small young planet in a large old universe. Moreover, lives lived out in environments, social as well as natural, that are distinctive even within the span of the single planet's existence. Distinctive also are the perceptual faculties and cognitive abilities that human inquirers have. These might have been different had evolution on Earth taken an alternate path and might sharply differ from those of other intelligent inquirers elsewhere in the universe, again if there be such.

Although complete liberation from such contingencies is not in the offing, it can be appropriate to try to shrink their influence, with the pressures to do so being all the greater when the goal is also to arrive at insights that are as non-indexical as possible, as is the case in the sciences. As mentioned earlier, the pressures in the humanities run in the opposite direction. The need for perspectival insights reinforces the need for indexical insights, and vice versa. Many of the issues of the humanities are so contextually situated that successful treatments of them have to include information about individuals and groups living in particular times and places. In addition, many of the issues are so entangled with human consciousness that accounts of them also have to include insights about the intentions, purposes, and points of views of the relevant individuals and groups, which are conditioned by their contexts and which inquirers try to access by extrapolating from their own experiences and histories.

There is no reason to think that human inquirers are in a privileged position with respect to issues of the basic sciences, but when it comes to the humanities, as the term itself might suggest, they have a leg up. They have firsthand understanding of what human conscious states and points of view are like, and what it is like to live in a human society. We humans tend to take this understanding for granted, but imagine once again that somewhere there are sophisticated inquirers with nonhuman faculties living in societies quite different from those of humans. No matter how intellectually gifted they may be, they would face far greater obstacles than we in coming to grips with those issues about human lives and societies that are deeply enmeshed with the conscious states and points of view of humans. For, we but not they can draw upon our own human-like experiences and histories living in human societies. This is just to say that in addressing such issues, we human inquirers can, do, and should take advantage of our distinctive ways of apprehending the world.

This is not the best approach for every issue about conscious states. Investigations into their origins and the neurophysiological conditions underlying them can try to be as non-perspectival as any other kind of scientific inquiry. That's not the rub. The problem, rather, is that insofar as some of the issues that interest us about conscious creatures require a degree of understanding what it is like to be the creature in question, what it is like to be a bat in a bat-like environment, to use Thomas Nagel's example,[8] even a complete as possible neurophysiological account of the creature's brain won't be of help. That's not what the account is supposed to be about.

The relevance of this point goes far beyond issues about the conscious states of bats. It extends also to the vast set of phenomena that arise only because there are conscious creatures in the world, especially a particular kind of conscious creature—humans. There is a dizzying array of social and cultural issues so thoroughly entangled with human experiences and purposes that satisfying treatments of them have to take into account what it is like to be these creatures, that is, what it is like to be a human. And when the issues concern specific individuals and groups, the treatments have to be also concerned with what it is (or was) like to be them.

All the issues cited earlier as representative of the humanities are examples. They are all intertwined with how humans experience the world and their points of view. Whether the topic is a history of the scientific and political efforts to battle the polio epidemic in the postwar period, or depictions of masculinity and femininity in

8. See Thomas Nagel, *Mortal Questions* (Cambridge: Cambridge University Press, 1979). Also Frank Jackson, "Epiphenomenal Qualia," *Philosophical Quarterly* 32 (1982): 127–136.

English and French romances in the late Middle Ages, or the history of Zionism in Soviet Russia of the 1920s, the insights being sought require not only an understanding of what it is to be human and to live in a human society but also specific insights about the experiences, purposes, and perceptions of the people and groups in question, insights, that is, about what it is (or was) like to be those particular humans in their particular circumstances.

There is no shortage of difficulties in grasping how the world seems to another conscious being, bats being a hard case, which is why Nagel chose them. Seeking insights about our fellow humans and their lives is not quite as daunting, since we have similar bodies and faculties and live in broadly comparable environments. So, there is a shared experiential and behavioral base for us to draw upon. There are still obstacles aplenty, of course. Human lives, points of views, and societies are notoriously complex and difficult to penetrate, and it is especially demanding to understand those far removed in time, distance, or culture. In a later section titled "Involvement with Mentality," I will be discussing in more detail the challenges of investigating phenomena that are deeply entangled with conscious states, but for now there are three general points to make.

The first is that although some of the issues of interest to us about humans do not require coming to grips with their conscious states and points of view, many do. There are insights to be had about humans and their societies that cannot be captured apart from details about how the people or groups in question experience their physical and social environments, and the ways in which these details affect their points of view and influence their behavior.

The second point is that in addressing such issues, human inquirers have an advantage. They know firsthand what human conscious states are like, and what it is to have a human point of view. They understand what it is for humans to see, hear, taste, smell, and touch. They also know from personal experience what it is for them to feel various emotions: anger, jealousy, regret, nervousness, irritation, admiration, compassion, love, and so on. In addition, from living in a human society they accrue a massive amount of information, which those not living in human societies would find it difficult to acquire, about characteristic human purposes, intentions, and behavior. Relying on all this, they make inferences about the conscious states and points of views of those who are their subjects and the various issues entwined with these states and points of view.

Difficult as it sometimes is to make these inferences, things get harder still in the humanities, where the project is to work up the inferences into accounts that will be illuminating to others. For then, it is necessary also to take into consideration the perspectives of the intended audience. The task facing inquirers is to mobilize enough of their own experiences, background information, concepts, and values that have overlaps with those of the audience to make intelligible to them the consciousness-inflected issues under study. The audience can be more or less broad, but unlike the sciences whose claims are ideally intended for a contextually unrestricted audience, in the humanities the audience is always limited. The emphasis is not on seeking results that will be as widely accessible as possible, certainly not to all creatures of comparable cognitive abilities, however different they and their circumstances may be. The primary goal is instead one of more local appropriation, to make the issues understandable to an "us"—our discipline, our society, our age, or whatever.

Consider efforts to make a past society understandable to a contemporary audience. The hope is to provide this audience with some understanding of how members of the past society conceived their environment, social as well as physical, and how they found their ways around it. Not that the account has to be bound by the views of its subjects. That's only a place to begin. Just as the significance of a text need not be exhausted by the author's intentions, so too the significance of historical events or periods need not be exhausted by the interpretations of the participants. It is not necessarily a debilitating flaw of a proposed account that the inhabitants of the society being investigated would not themselves have endorsed or perhaps even understood it. Insight for the contemporary audience is what counts·

But audiences are not fixed in stone. They change. So, it is not to be expected that even highly successful accounts will continue to be helpful for future generations. As the home society changes, so too does the information needed for understanding. The civilization of the classical period of Ancient Greece has special resonance for European influenced societies, since many of the cherished assumptions and traditions of these societies have their roots in this period. Within these societies, however, different eras have understood classical Greek civilization and their relationships to it in different ways. There is every reason to think, moreover, that these reinterpretations will continue. The dynamic of successive generations arriving at their own understanding of an iconic society (e.g., classical Greece), event (e.g., the French Revolution), piece of literature (e.g., Hamlet), or work of art (e.g., Rembrandt's self-portraits) is a familiar feature of the landscape of the humanities.

The upshot is that for the consciousness-suffused issues that are of central concern to the humanities, not only must inquirers not try to minimize perspectival considerations, they need to be triply occupied with them. "Triply" because three distinct sets of perspectives are relevant: those of the people, societies, or times under investigation, those of the intended audience, and their own.

Which brings me to the third point: the sciences, especially the basic sciences, push in the opposite direction. There the aim is to escape to the extent possible the idiosyncrasies of the inquirer's and the audience's perspectives. Moreover, the issues for the most part do not concern conscious phenomena, but even when they do, the most sought-after accounts of them are based on information outside the sphere of what is inflected with consciousness and perspective, information, for example, about the neurophysiological conditions associated with conscious states and processes.

Again, I will be returning to these issues in the section titled "Involvement with Mentality," but even this is enough to see that there is a trade-off that confronts the humanities and sciences alike when dealing with consciousness-related issues. To the extent that inquirers make minimal use of indexical and perspectival elements, they potentially may make their results accessible to others in a wider range of circumstances, but they are foregoing investigative approaches that are especially well suited for understanding phenomena entangled with the experiences, purposes, and intentions of people living at particular times and places. Furthermore, to the extent that inquirers make liberal use of perspectival and indexical factors at their disposal, they may put themselves in a better position to generate insights about these phenomena, but by the same token they invariably find themselves addressing a contextually located and hence more restricted audience.

The sciences and humanities deal with this trade-off differently. The choice each makes is fully defensible, given the kind of insights being sought, but there is also a cost. By its choice, each finds itself ill-positioned to address certain questions, since different kinds of questions call for different kinds of inquiry and produce different kinds of insights. This division may produce feelings of discomfort about whether and how all the insights fit into a higher order framework. There is an understandable impulse not to be content with distinct types of knowledge that are not systematically related within a larger unified conception. We want there to be an encompassing worldview, a single, grounding metaphysics.

Many are convinced that it has to be a materialist one, which regards all things in the universe, including all the diverse expressions of human consciousness found in human societies, as grounded in complex physical and biological processes acting in accordance with fundamental laws, although there are, to be sure, different views about what the exact nature of this grounding might be. A rival to materialism in all its forms, and a more traditional view, is that some kind of theistic metaphysics is needed to provide the unifying, higher order framework, where once again there are competing views about what form this theism should take. There are also those who think that neither materialism nor theism will do and that some third alternative, which we are not yet in a position to conceive adequately, is necessary.[9]

I sympathize with the desire for a single, higher order conception and grant that trying to develop it is an important project, but this is not my project. The central theme of this work is that at least for now, different approaches are necessary for understanding different issues. This may sit uneasily with those who want to insist that there just has to be a single best way of understanding everything, with the not-so-hidden corollary that inquiries have no standing unless they can be vindicated in terms of the privileged form of understanding.

The "there just has to be," however, is more of a wish than a finding, and the charitable thing to say about it is that it is premature. Perhaps someday we may know how to deploy a single framework to address all the questions that interest us, but we do not yet know

9. See Thomas Nagel, *Mind and Cosmos* (Oxford: Oxford University Press, 2012); and Colin McGinn, *The Problem of Consciousness* (London: Basil Blackwell, 1991).

how to do so. For the moment, there is no choice but to live with different kinds of inquiry and different kinds of insights. As for the fear that in the end they might not fit together, the flippant but correct response is that they somehow do, because there is only one world, not two. This may sound trivial, but it is not. It has implications. It means, for one, that there is no impenetrable firewall between the sciences and the humanities. There is instead a continuum, with the features distinguishing the two coming in degrees and their home issues touching upon one another.

There is also no basis for either to ignore or discount the other. Science cannot think of itself as being without limits, as if its methods were the most suitable ones for all that interests us, but neither can the humanities conceive themselves as autonomous from the sciences, as if the latter's results can be safely disregarded when addressing issues in the humanities. In the section titled "An Endpoint to Inquiry," I will be suggesting that a characteristic mark of the humanities is that there usually can be no stopping place for inquiries into its issues, since over time new circumstances can and regularly do force reconsideration of previously reached views. Among these new circumstances is new scientific knowledge— again, more on this later.

PRESCRIPTIVE VS. DESCRIPTIVE

Prescriptive claims give expression to values, while descriptive claims profess to report facts. The former are about what should be the case, while the latter are about what is the case. Like the other distinctions, this one is not all-or-nothing. Many claims have both descriptive and prescriptive content, sometimes so deeply intermingled as to be virtually inseparable. To assess someone's behavior as cowardly is to make a negative evaluation of it, but it also has descriptive implications. Not all bad acts are cowardly, only ones that involve helpless victims or excessive fear or the like. "Thick" terms such as cowardly stand in contrast to "thin" ones such as "bad" or "wrong," which also negatively assess behavior but do so without entailing much if anything in the way of a non-evaluative description of it. Complex ethical and political issues are also thick. Coming to grips with capital punishment, human genetic selection, or environmental responsibilities to future generations involves dealing with a host of factual as well as evaluative considerations.[10]

Questions about the status of prescriptive claims are as old as philosophy itself and still vigorously debated,[11] but for my purposes what matters are two general, non-nihilistic theses, which are widely, if not universally, accepted. The first is that there is some distinction or another to be made between the descriptive and the prescriptive. Explaining what it amounts to has proven to be controversial, but however tricky it is to distinguish the descriptive from the prescriptive, it has to be admitted when all is said and done that, say, Mill's position on freedom of speech is more prescriptive and less

---

10. See Bernard Williams's discussion of thick and thin moral concepts in his *Ethics and the Limits of Philosophy* (Cambridge, MA: Harvard University Press, 1985).

11. For a sampling of recent literature, see Simon Blackburn, *Essays in Quasi-Realism* (Oxford: Oxford University Press, 1993); Alan Gibbard, *Wise Choices, Apt Feelings* (Cambridge, MA: Harvard University Press, 1990); Christine Korsgaard, *The Sources of Normativity* (New York: Cambridge University Press, 1996); Thomas Nagel, *The View from Nowhere* (Oxford: Oxford University, 1986); Derek Parfit, *On What Matters* (Oxford: Oxford University Press, 2011); Geoffrey Sayre-McCord, *Essays on Moral Realism* (Ithaca, NY: Cornell University Press, 1998); T. M. Scanlon, *What We Owe to Each Other* (Cambridge, MA: Harvard University Press, 1998); Sharon Street, "Constructivism about Reasons," in *Oxford Studies in Metaethics*, vol. 3, ed. Russ Shafer-Landau (Oxford: Clarendon Press, 2008), 207–245; Sharon Street, "In Defense of Future Tuesday Indifference: Ideally Coherent Eccentrics and the Contingency of What Matters," *Philosophical Issues* 19, Metaethics (2009): 273–297; and Bernard Williams, *Moral Luck* (Cambridge: Cambridge University Press, 1981).

descriptive than Newton's laws of motion. The second thesis is that there are standards for assessing prescriptive claims. What exactly they are and how they are determined is contested, but once more almost everyone acknowledges that prescriptive claims meeting the relevant standards are superior to those that do not. They are either more accurate, or more coherent, or more fitting, or in some other way more defensible.

It follows that individuals can have better or worse understanding of prescriptive issues, and it can be an aim or inquiry to increase this understanding. This cannot be the primary responsibility of scientific inquiries, however. To be sure, the sciences do generate information that is important to have in deliberating about "thick" ethical and political issues, but when doing so, their contribution is descriptive. Background knowledge about gravity is needed to assess how efficiently gravity-induced tides might be harnessed in tidal turbines to generate energy, but there is a thicket of political and ethical considerations that need to be addressed for this information to have implications for environmental policy. The theory of gravity is of help "only" in providing an accurate understanding of the strengths and frequencies of tides on Earth, not for insights about how or whether they ought to be harnessed for energy in lieu of other sources. One can always fantasize about gravity being a stronger force than it is and hence producing stronger and potentially more utilizable tides on Earth, but this is the stuff of science fiction, not science. The aim of science, to repeat, is to be descriptive.

The sciences do make extensive use of idealizations, however. The ideal gas law describes the relationship of pressure, volume, and temperature of gases under conditions that never perfectly obtain. In particular, it makes simplifying assumptions about the molecules making up gases, for example, they do not attract or repel one another and do not themselves take up volume. The molecules of real gases are not like this, but their behavior is nonetheless close enough to ideal ones that the gas law is useful. Indeed, there are philosophers of science who argue that this is the best way to think about scientific theories in general; they are best regarded as models that are precisely accurate only under conditions that are never entirely realized.[12] Even on such views, however, the theories are still meant to be descriptive. They are to be used to make predictions and offer explanations about the behavior of gases or whatever phenomena are at issue in real situations. There are, accordingly, constraints as to how idealized they can be. They cannot be so far removed from real world systems as to be worthless in describing actual phenomena with acceptable degrees of accuracy.

The humanities also have descriptive aims. An account of the Battle of Waterloo seeks to depict elements of the battle—the sizes of the opposing forces, their weaponry, their positions, and so forth—that explain why it unfolded as it did. Similarly for projects about the roles played by canals and trains in the Industrial Revolution or the uses of meter in different traditions of poetry—here too the aim is accurate, detailed descriptions.

Although there is nothing in principle preventing inquiries in the humanities from being wholly concerned with descriptive matters, they often have prescriptive aspirations as well. Thus, it is not unusual or in any way out of place for a historian whose topic is the Battle of Waterloo also to weigh in on the wisdom of Napoleon's various military decisions, for example, his decision to wait until noon before engaging the battle, given that it had rained heavily the night before. These evaluations, in turn, involve value judgments

---

12. Ronald Giere, *Science without Laws* (Chicago: University of Chicago Press, 1999); and Nancy Cartwright, *How the Laws of Physics Lie* (Oxford: Oxford University Press, 1983).

about such issues as whether he was sufficiently open to non-conventional tactics that might have been more successful given the conditions.[13] So too it is with other studies in the humanities, from those assessing T. S. Eliot's stature as a twentieth-century poet to ones appraising the trade-offs Lincoln agreed to in order to get the Emancipation Proclamation passed. Descriptive accuracy is a prerequisite of such projects, but they are also interested in reaching evaluative conclusions.

In addition, there are projects in the humanities where the prescriptive elements dominate. Some of these, in the tradition of Aristotle's *Nicomachean Ethics,* make recommendations about how best to live one's life. Others, such as John Rawls's *A Theory of Justice* make proposals about justifiable kinds of political systems. Still others articulate principles for how best to think about art or literature. These works endorse views about what should be valued: a certain way of living, a particular kind of political structure, or a specific way to approach art and literature.

The sciences, by contrast, avoid making proposals about what should be valued, which is not to say that values do not motivate scientific inquiry. They obviously do. Science is a human activity, and like any other there is a mixed bag of reasons for engaging in it, ranging from sheer curiosity or lofty ethical aspirations to personal aggrandizement, but whatever the motivations, the insights themselves are intended to be descriptive and are to be evaluated as such.

This is an elementary but important distinction. A polymer chemist may be drawn to researching the synthesis of polymers by the prospects of developing improved materials for medicine,

---

13. See, e.g., Tim Clayton, *Four Days that Changed Europe's Destiny* (Boston: Little Brown, 2014); and Rory Muir, *Waterloo and the Fortunes of Peace* (New Haven, CT: Yale University Press, 2015).

which in turn would make for longer and better human lives, while a plant biologist may be inspired to study the genetic, cellular, and molecular biology of the Arabidopsis plant in hopes of improving the efficiency of agriculture, which could then help to reduce world hunger. But whatever the original motivation is for such work, once inquiry has begun, the imperative is for moral, political, and other such considerations to drop out and not affect the results. The aim of the work should then be descriptive, that of arriving at accurate conclusions about the synthesis in polymers or gene regulation in Arabidopsis. Not that there are not instances in the history of science, including notorious ones, where the surrounding political or religious climate did influence conclusions that were generally accepted in the scientific community. These are warning flags. We now see that past science was sometimes contaminated by such factors, and so too it may be with some of contemporary science.

It is not surprising, then, that there can be debates about the extent to which a current scientific view has been influenced by extraneous considerations. Whatever one makes of these disputes, it needs to be admitted that critiques of this general sort have the potential to be powerful. A core ideal of the sciences is to be descriptive. So, it is always a serious charge that their conclusions have been significantly shaped by moral, political, religious, or self-interested agendas.

Notice, however, that even if it could be shown that science as it is actually conducted is frequently at odds with this ideal, this would not show that there is anything wrong with the ideal itself. A different kind of argument would be needed for that, and it is hard to see what it would be, given that the ideal is not peculiar to science. It is one that governs other projects with descriptive aims, even ones far removed from the practices of science.

Suppose I am concerned whether I am saving enough and hence should be cutting down on expenses. Before trying to reach any decision about this, I resolve to collect information about the amount of funds in my various accounts (checking, savings, etc.), my debts (mortgage, other loans, credit cards, etc.), and the value of my disposable property (house, car, etc.). My task, like scientific ones, has a descriptive aim. The point is to arrive at an accurate overview of my current financial situation, without being influenced at this fact-finding stage by what I might like it to be.

How much time, effort, and care to devote to tasks of this sort is a separate question, the answer to which depends on how valuable the resulting information would be relative to the other things I care about. To illustrate with an extreme example, I could devote most of my waking hours going to the houses of friends and counting the number of grains of salt in their saltshakers. By doing so, I would be acquiring information I now lack, but such a project would be ill-conceived and even disturbing, since for any remotely normal person, the value of the information being acquired is so out of line with the time and effort needed to obtain it.

The issue here is a familiar one of resource allocation, the economics of inquiry, as it were. There are always choices to be made, whether in science or everyday life, about what information it would be useful to have and the amount of time, effort, and expense it is fitting to devote to acquiring it. If these choices are made badly, the resulting inquiry, even if successful on its own terms, may not generate much of real significance.

All this can be acknowledged, however, without any retreat from the view that the aim of scientific inquiry should be descriptive. Pragmatic, political, and ethical values give direction to science by indicating what kinds of information it would be valuable to acquire. In addition, they impose constraints by indicating how much time, effort, and other resources it makes sense to expend. They also constrain the ways in which evidence can be acquired, for example, restrictions on the appropriate treatment of humans and animals in experiments and trials. Once the direction and constraints are established, however, the project should be to reach conclusions that are accurate. To be sure, there are values governing this project as well, ones of thoroughness, impartiality, consistency, and the like, but these are the values of descriptive inquiry. They are in the service to the goal of reaching conclusions that are accurate, not ones that accord with a preferred set of pragmatic, political, or ethical ends.

By contrast, it can be altogether appropriate for inquiries in the humanities to aim at prescriptive insights as well as descriptive ones. They can be focused on arriving at assessments of a historical figure's virtues as a political leader, or the merits of a piece of literature, or the positive and negative effects of a social movement. To reach conclusions about these matters, humanities scholars have to enter into the realm of the prescriptive. They need to make value judgments. They can be criticized for how they do so. They may be basing their evaluation on sloppily acquired information, or biases may be causing them to ignore relevant facts, or they may be giving undue weight to relatively inconsequential factors. The criticism, however, cannot simply be that ethical, political, or other values have had a major influence on the conclusions reached, since about these issues, there is no alternative but to appeal to such values.

INDIVIDUAL VS. COLLECTIVE

You need to leave for the airport by 7:30, and you are not wearing a watch. You look at the clock on the wall, unaware that it has stopped, and come to believe it is quarter past seven. By chance, it actually is quarter past seven, but you do not know this to be the case.

A banal example but one with a lesson. To know something, you need to be right about it, but you also need to have enough neighboring information. "Enough" is vague by design. "The whole truth and nothing but the truth" is a familiar oath, but we have to be satisfied with less, given that there are endless truths associated with every situation, even seemingly simple ones like that of a stopped clock on the wall. The clock is a certain size. Its housing is made of plastic that is a particular shade of off-white. It is fastened to a wall that has been painted a light grey color. The paint on the wall is latex, not oil-based. The wall is in a room whose dimensions are 19 feet in length, 15 feet in width, and 10 feet in height. It has three windows. There are also historical truths about the situation. The clock was bought online twelve months ago and was delivered by a Fed Ex truck. There are negative truths as well. The face of the clock is not square, and there are no dogs in the room—nor are there camels or peacocks.

Every situation brims over with truths, but our information is always limited. No matter how thorough we are, there are gaps in our information, but not all gaps are equal. Many of the truths we lack are not worth having. When you look at the clock on the wall to get the time, you are unlikely to care whether the wall was painted with latex as opposed to oil-based paint. But, sometimes the information we lack is important, as when you need to leave for the airport by a certain time but are unaware that the clock you're looking at has stopped. To have knowledge about something is to have information about it that is accurate and comprehensive enough given the context.[14]

14. For more on this way of thinking about knowledge, see Richard Foley, *When Is True Belief Knowledge?* (Princeton, NJ: Princeton University Press, 2012).

Collective knowledge has many of these same features. Something is part of the collective knowledge of a group only if there is a consensus within the group about its truth and the group also has enough information about it. Not just any group of people can be said to have collective knowledge, however. It is nonsensical to ask what individuals who have green eyes, live in the northern hemisphere, and whose birthdate is in September collectively know. They do not have the necessary social links and joint purposes. Exactly what these links and purposes have to be is an intriguing question, but the more pressing issue for purposes here is that there can be different ways to arrive at a consensus, however the group is defined.

The most obvious way is for enough individuals in the group to ascertain on their own that the claim in question is true. But, even when only a few individuals are in a position to determine its truth firsthand, something can still be collectively believed and known if these few have the requisite intellectual authority and have vouched for it. This route to consensus and collective knowledge is especially important in scientific fields that are so technical that only a small number of highly trained individuals are in a position to understand the work being done. Breakthroughs by them can nonetheless expand the collective stock of knowledge available to the broader scientific community.

The relevant community includes future as well as current inquirers. Building over time on the discoveries of one's predecessors is one of the most familiar features of the history of science. Kepler's contributions to astronomy in the seventeenth-century were possible only because of the earlier work of Copernicus, Tycho Brahe, and many others. Kepler's discoveries then put subsequent investigators such as Robert Hooke and Isaac Newton in a position to make their contributions.

The American philosopher C. S. Peirce was among the first to highlight the importance of thinking about science in terms of a temporally extended community of inquirers. His view was that the ultimate goal of scientific inquiry should be a definitive account of whatever is being investigated, but given the relatively early stage of modern science and short life spans of humans, it is usually not realistic for individual scientists to achieve this goal on their own, at least not for large topics. Pierce concluded that as a condition of their rationality, scientists must view themselves as part of a community of inquirers that will continue its work well into the future. For, it is only by identifying themselves with such a community and focusing on their roles in adding to its collective stock of knowledge that there is a realistic chance of achieving what ought to be their goal.

"The method of modern science is social in respect to the solidarity of its efforts. The scientific world is like a colony of insects in that the individual strives to produce that which he cannot himself hope to enjoy. One generation collects premises in order that a distant generation may discover what they mean. When a problem comes before the scientific world, a hundred men immediately set their energies to work on it. One contributes this, another that. Another company, standing on the shoulders of the first, strikes a little higher until at last the parapet is attained."[15]

Peirce may have been exaggerating for effect when he compared scientists to a colony of insects. He also may have been insufficiently appreciative that arriving at definitive accounts of what is being investigated is more of an ideal toward which progress can be made as opposed to an end that is always fully achievable. Still, these

---

15. *Collected Papers of Charles Sanders Peirce*, ed. C. Hartshorne, P. Weiss, and A. Burks (Cambridge, MA: Harvard University Press, 1931-1958), 7:87.

quibbles aside, he was onto something. Science is at its heart a collective enterprise, although to be sure, one driven forward by individual effort and achievement.

The key mechanism for incorporating individual contributions into the collective enterprise is the division of intellectual labor. Reduced to its bare bones, the system works by breaking up problems into components, encouraging investigators to develop highly refined expertise in these narrowly defined areas, and then requiring them to make their research publicly available, so that their findings can not only be verified by others but also used by them, and used even by those who are not themselves in a position to defend the findings.

A widely noted consequence of specialization in the sciences is that non-scientists, even highly educated ones, lack the training and background knowledge needed to understand the work in specialized fields. Authorities on Renaissance literature are not in a position to comprehend, much less assess, string theory. This was at the heart of C. P. Snow's anxieties about the relationship between the humanities and the sciences.[16] What is less frequently noted is that most fellow scientists are not in a much better position. Biologists also lack the training and background needed to assess developments in string theory, and for that matter, so do most other physicists. Correspondingly, string theorists are not especially well placed to evaluate advanced work in molecular genetics, and neither are geologists.

One of the significant changes in intellectual life over the last hundred years or so is the growing disparity between what is collectively known and what individuals have the capacity and training to understand and assess on their own. The widening of this

16. C. P. Snow, *The Two Cultures* (Cambridge: Cambridge University Press, 2012).

gap has social, political, and educational implications of great consequence, but the point of immediate interest is the more restricted one that science at its heart is an enterprise organized to expand what is collectively known, whereas collective knowledge plays a less central and institutionalized role in the humanities. Not that they too are not communal enterprises. The fields making up the humanities and the standards for conducting inquiry in them have been developed over time by generations of scholars. Insights coming out of these inquiries are thus not simply the products of solitary individuals doing their work in seclusion. They are also the products of social practices that have been collectively constructed.

There are many other communal aspects of the humanities as well. Scholars rely on research done by peers, past and present. They make use of archival materials that have been collected and preserved by others. There are schools of thought that urge the use of preferred methodologies, and movements that direct inquirers toward neglected areas of research. There are also cooperative efforts of a more limited sort, for example, anthologies, book series, and conferences. And in a later section on intellectual progress, I will be describing some ways that fields in the humanities can be said to make collective progress.

This being said, in the humanities, consensus and collective knowledge do not play the defining roles they do in the sciences. Nor is there nearly as much pressure to arrive at consensus. The sciences have more sharply defined practical aims than the humanities. The project is not just to understand the world but also to control it. Science goes hand in hand with engineering and technology, with the former being the supplier of information for the latter, but to carry out their projects, engineers and technicians need to be able to draw upon a collectively agreed-upon stock of information.

Consensus does not come easily even in the sciences, but it is facilitated by the requirement that hypotheses be formulated so that they are falsified if predicted observations do not turn out as expected. Agreement that a proposed hypothesis is false is not enough to create accord on what is true, but with repeated use over time, efforts to disconfirm can and often do produce agreement about where the truth lies, or at least its approximate vicinity. Agreement is a relative term, of course. It is not as if everyone has to concur. Indeed, in any intellectual community, there are benefits to tolerating contrarian views. As John Stuart Mill was eager to emphasize, uniformity of opinion can even be a sign that coercive social pressures are at work.[17] Some of these may have been deliberately designed to encourage conformity of opinion, while others may have been unplanned but still lead to "group think." Likewise, some may exercise their influence widely, while others operate locally, affecting only a small community of individuals.

As an example of the latter, the philosopher Roderick Chisholm, who taught for many years at Brown University, had his own way of producing consensus in his seminars. At the first meeting, he would propose a general, usually uncontroversial, principle about the philosophical topic being discussed and ask for objections to it. Once the seminar participants were satisfied that the principle was acceptable, he would move on to a second principle, again inviting objections, before moving on to the next. He repeated the procedure at subsequent meetings and in this way over the course of the semester built up an impressively complex list of interrelated principles, with each addition making the overall system a little more consequential. It was a rule of the seminar, however, that once a principle was accepted,

---

17. J. S. Mill, "Of the Liberty of Thought and Discussion," in *On Liberty and Other Writings*, ed. S. Collini (Cambridge: Cambridge University Press, 1989).

students were not allowed later to return to it and raise objections. This rule, Chisholm insisted, was necessary for making progress, but bold students would occasionally become obstinate about giving their blessings to a principle even if they could not immediately formulate objections to it. Their fear, a wholly justified one, was that it might later be wielded against them in ways that they could not yet foresee. If as a result the discussion threatened to get bogged down, Chisholm would call for a vote by the seminar participants on whether the principle being discussed was acceptable or not. If the majority voted "yes," it would be added to the collective stock that was available to deal with the issues and could not be later challenged; if the majority said "no," the seminar would continue to consider revisions until the majority, either from persuasion or exhaustion, gave its OK.

Here then was a mechanism for producing a local consensus, but it was obviously a joke consensus, and Chisholm's amused manner on such occasions indicated that he intended it to be such. Its jokey quality derived from the awareness that normally there should not be much room for deference in philosophy, and certainly not deference to a majority vote. The objective of inquiries in philosophy, and the same is true across the other humanities, has to have a more individualistic flavor, and "individualistic" in a couple of distinct but related senses. First, individual insight is to be sought and highly valued even when it is not helpful in achieving a consensus. For many topics of importance in the humanities, agreement is not to be expected or for that matter even encouraged. Second, there is a more individualistic aspect about the way in which influence should be exercised. The primary goal should be to put others in a position to understand, appreciate, and defend for themselves the insights in question, whether these are ones about a philosophical principle, the moral defensibility of the trade-offs Lincoln agreed to in order to end slavery, or the aesthetic merits of T. S. Eliot as a poet.

The most important role for experts in the humanities is that of exerting Socratic influence, not intellectual authority. Suppose you get me to believe a claim through a series of well thought-out questions and instructions. Afterwards, I understand what you understand and believe what you believe, but my believing it is no longer dependent upon you. I now understand it on my own and am able to defend it on my own. You have exercised Socratic influence over me but not authority.[18]

Like the other distinctions being discussed, this one is not black or white. It is often a mixture of deference and firsthand understanding that leads someone to accept the conclusions of another. More generally, it has to be acknowledged that all of us rely constantly and continuously on the opinions of others for the information that we need or simply interests us, indeed so much that we are all, as the historian Marc Bloch once memorably expressed the point, "permanently floating in a soup of deference" to others.[19] It begins in earliest infancy, accelerates throughout childhood, and continues through adulthood until the end of life. The opinions of others envelop us: family, friends, acquaintances, colleagues, strangers, books, articles, media, and now websites, blogs, and tweets. Much of what we believe invariably comes from what others have said or written. There is no escape. No escape in one's everyday life, no escape in one's work life, and if one is a scholar, no escape in one's scholarly life.

So, the claim here is not that deference to others has no place whatsoever in the humanities. It obviously does, and I will be discussing how and when it does so in chapter 3, the section titled

18. The term "Socratic influence" is from Alan Gibbard, *Wise Choices, Apt Feelings* (Cambridge, MA: Harvard University Press, 1990).

19. Marc Bloch, "Rituals and Deference," in *Rituals and Memory: Towards a Comparative Anthropology of Religion*, ed. H. Whitehouse and J. Laidlaw (London: Altamira Press, 2004).

"Intellectual Authority." Nor is the claim that Socratic influence has no role in the sciences. I will be discussing this in more detail in that chapter as well. But for now, the lesson is simply that in the humanities there is nothing like the organized system of specialization and deference to the views of the experts that one finds in the sciences, and likewise nowhere near the overall emphasis on arriving at a consensus. Correspondingly, individual insight is more highly valued for its own sake, independently of its ability to contribute to a collective agenda.

Chapter 3

Secondary Differences

AN ENDPOINT TO INQUIRY

The sciences value knowledge that is collective, nonindexical, non-perspectival, and descriptive. The humanities depart from the sciences in one or more of these ways, emphasizing knowledge that is individual, indexical, perspectival, and/or prescriptive. These features can be thought of as providing broadly drawn intellectual maps of the two domains. The contrasts between the maps can then be heightened with the addition of distinctive secondary features. In the following sections, I discuss some of the more important of these secondary differences, which like the primary ones are intertwined with one another.

The first difference is that inquiries in the sciences but not the humanities are designed to move over time in the direction of definitive accounts of their issues—accounts that are accurate and comprehensive, and on which there is consensus. There do not have to be realistic prospects for reaching this point anytime soon or, for that matter, in the foreseeable future. A definitive account can nonetheless function as an ideal. As with other ideals that cannot be perfectly realized, it is enough that there be movement toward it.

Even this is not easy and is by no means inevitable, but there are practices to facilitate it. A key one, as mentioned earlier, is that hypotheses are expected to be formulated in ways that can be used to predict observable outcomes, which when not forthcoming tend to disconfirm them. This is "tend to disconfirm" because as W. V. O. Quine pointed out, if one is willing to make enough revisions in background assumptions, one can always protect a favored view.[1] In actual practice, however, hypotheses do get disconfirmed when predictions fail, and this is one way of fostering consensus. Agreement on what is false does not ensure agreement on what is true, but it does narrow the field; and with continued use over time, it can generate consensus for where the truth lies, or since accuracy and comprehensiveness can come in degrees, for at least its general vicinity.

Because there are countless truths associated with any situation, event, or phenomenon, and hence it is never possible to be aware of all of them, converging on an account that is accurate and comprehensive implies "only" that most of the important truths about the issue are known. And even if all the important truths were known, there still might be opportunities for other kinds of improvements. An ideal account would also minimize indexicality by providing an accurate treatment of the phenomena in question, not just for a limited set of times and places but for all times and places, or as close to this as is possible. In addition, it would employ a minimum of perspectival elements and would be as elegantly formulated as possible, thus increasing the chances that those with different perspectives might be able to understand it. If an account managed to be ideal in all these ways, there would be no intellectual reasons to modify it.

1. Willard V. O. Quine, "Two Dogmas of Empiricism," in *From a Logical Point of View*, 2nd ed. (Cambridge, MA: Harvard University Press, 2006), 37–46.

Political, social, or other extraneous reasons might still trigger revisions, but there wouldn't be room for intellectual improvements.

Not for humans, at any rate. It is possible that our collective life span will not be long enough for us to have full understanding of some matters. Nor does it help that we have observational access to only a tiny speck of the universe. Add the built-in limitations of human cognitive abilities, and it begins to seem that there might well be features of the universe we humans will never understand with the degree of accuracy and comprehensiveness that a superior species of inquirers might achieve. Be this as it may, if a theory were as accurate and comprehensive as is humanly possible for it to be, minimally indexical and perspectival, and also as elegantly formulated as possible, it would be a natural stopping point for us.

More cautiously, it would appear to be such. This caution is needed, because there are never absolute guarantees of the accuracy of any theory. I discuss why this is so and its implications in the concluding chapter ("A Plea for Intellectual Humility"), but for now its relevance is that, absent complete certainty, it is conceivable that unanticipated new evidence will reopen questions thought to have been settled. Still, over time the probability of major surprises can become increasingly remote, and as such, inquiry into the issue would approach a stopping point.

But a final proviso is needed, namely that this is so only for theoretical inquiry. Efforts to find new applications need not come to an end. Science is occupied not just with understanding the world but also with using its knowledge to achieve practical ends. So, even if a theoretical endpoint were approached, technological advances making new uses of the knowledge remain possible. It's just that there would not be reasons to think that anything will necessitate significant revisions of the underlying theory.

There are some who even maintain that the basic sciences are already approaching such an endpoint. They argue that advances in physics, chemistry, and biology during the past several centuries have been so immense that future discoveries are bound to be minor in comparison. Existing theories may be refined a bit, and there will certainly be developments in technology, but nothing will force major changes in their basic description of reality. Current theories have this pretty much right.[2]

Whether or not this is a plausible view is debatable, but no matter. What counts for our purposes here is that, however closely one thinks some of the sciences may be approaching definitive treatments of their issues, it is fitting for them to try to make advances toward this goal, whereas in the humanities this usually is not a suitable goal at all. For most of its issues, the notion of a conclusive account that settles matters once and for all cannot function as an ideal—not even one that might be approached asymptotically in the long run. Inquiries are instead open ended in the sense that major additional insights and revisions are always possible, always to be expected, and always to be sought.

The prescriptive, indexical, and perspectival nature of issues in the humanities combines to make this so, but the open-endedness of its inquiries is perhaps most readily apparent when the issues have significant prescriptive elements, as many in the humanities do. So, let's begin with them. Suppose an aspect of the situation being investigated involves questions about how the individuals involved might best have dealt with conflicts between responsibilities to their families and friends and those owed to their country, strangers, and humanity in general. Think of accounts of the Nazi occupation of France during World War II, and the hard choices faced by many

2. See John Horgan, *The End of Science* (Reading, MA: Addison-Wesley, 1996).

French citizens during this period. Progressing toward a definitive account of the attraction that physical bodies exert on one another is a coherent if difficult goal to pursue, but this is not a plausible goal for inquiries into issues involving loyalties and responsibilities to family, friends, country, and humanity.

What would a definitive account of these issues look like? Might it be one that proposes a fundamental ethical principle and then derives from it decisive conclusions about how individuals in their concrete situations should have dealt with the issues of loyalty and responsibility they faced? Not likely. Over the long history of philosophical ethics, none of the principles put forward as fundamental has produced anything like general agreement. And, even if agreement were somehow reached, there would remain a huge gap between the generality of the principle and the specificity of the situations in which decisions have to be made. If the principles are to be universal, they have to have a very general form. According to Mill, the first principle is to do that which will maximize utility, while according to Kant, it is to act in accordance with maxims that can be universalized. Principles of this degree of generality, however, cannot be used to generate definitive solutions to the problems that individuals often face in concrete situations.

Jean-Paul Sartre, among others, took notice of this gap and used his skills as a storyteller to dramatize it. One of his stories focused on this very issue: how obligations to family and friends can be in tension with obligations to one's country or humankind in general. He recounts how a young man in occupied France was grappling with the choice of whether to remain in France and care for his ailing mother or to join the Free French forces assembling in England to fight the Nazis. As Sartre tells his story, the youth was fully aware that by staying with his mother he could be sure of aiding her in what were likely her final years, whereas anything he might do in going to fight might well "vanish like water into sand and serve no purpose." His was an agonizing dilemma, and yet none of the standard ethical theories, whether utilitarian or Kantian or any other, was capable of resolving it definitively in favor of one choice over the other.[3]

Sartre linked the lack of clear-cut resolutions to such problems with his critique of the idea of objective values in general. An alternative way to think about such cases is that they illustrate the need to abandon the "value monism" that is implicit in a search for a single first principle of ethics. The complexities of real-life decisions are resistant to being captured by any single value, whether value is understood objectively or subjectively. In difficult situations, there are instead multiple values to be balanced, with no general recipe for how best to balance them. Coming to grips with these situations has the character, to use Ronald Dworkin's image, of running from value to value in search of other values. Nor, as Dworkin also emphasizes, is it possible to opt out of disputes with others about difficult ethical and political situations by declaring "We just disagree, and there's nothing more to say," for this, too, is a claim that is appropriate to debate. [4] One of the characteristic marks of prescriptive issues is that there are always ways for the willing to continue the conversation, but this remains a possibility precisely because there is never a question of there being a final, definitive account of the issues.

The indexical character of the insights being sought is an additional reason why there generally can be no thought of getting closer and closer to an endpoint of inquiry. The humanities are concerned with issues associated with humans living in particular places and times—issues that by their very nature are highly indexical.

3. J. P. Sartre, *Existentialism is a Humanism* (New Haven, CT: Yale University Press, 2007).
4. Ronald Dworkin, *Justice for Hedgehogs* (Cambridge, MA: Harvard University Press, 2011).

Satisfactory accounts of these issues inevitably must have an index-ical cast as well, although there is always room for debate about the degree of indexicality best suited to produce insights.

The illustration given in the section "Indexical vs. Non-Indexical (chapter 4) is that some historians in their search for historical understanding fix on a few prominent individuals or events, oth-ers on the details of everyday life, still others on political ideas or economics forces, and yet others on more long-term factors, such as climate and diversity of plant and animal life. They choose a dimension they think is most important in making the past under-standable, but there is no single best way of making these choices, nor would there be much point in trying to settle upon one, since the various approaches can co-exist and even complement one another. All of this further confirms that ordinarily there is nothing like a natural stopping point for inquiries about the past. For some sharply defined descriptive questions, such as the details of a partic-ular event (its time, location, participants, etc.) or the provenance of a painting or manuscript, it may be possible to arrive at some-thing approaching a definitive answer; but in general, with efforts to understand the past, there always remain open questions about where the focus should be, how far back to go, and how broadly or narrowly to look.

The perspectival character of the insights is a third factor that tends to preclude any thought of arriving at an endpoint for inquiry. Many of the issues in the humanities are such that satisfying accounts of them have to be perspectival—indeed, as pointed out previously, must be multi-perspectival. The points of views of the inquirers and those who are the subjects of the study come into play, but so do those of the audience. The task facing inquirers is to com-municate information, concepts, values, and experiences to their audiences in ways that make the targeted subjects and their points of view comprehensible. There is progress to be made on issues of this sort (more on this in the next chapter), but it cannot be conceived as converging on a final, fixed account, if for no other reason than that audiences and their circumstances change.

Suppose the goal of a study is to help a society understand its own attitudes about the arts. It cannot be presumed that whatever insights are reached on these matters will continue to be useful as that society changes. As future generations begin to regard the current society as distant and unfamiliar, the information they will need in order to comprehend the current society's attitudes about the arts will be different from what is now used. So, it is not as if the aim can be to develop an account with no reasons for ever supplementing or revising.

It is no different for investigations into the history, politics, economics, arts, or religion of a past civilization. Here, too, there can be no thought of progressing toward to a conclusive account, since once again the audience will change over time. It thus has to be recognized in advance that even the most successful accounts will be in need of periodic renewal. Recall the efforts of successive generations of Western societies to come to grips with Classical Greek culture and their relationships to it.

The open-ended character of its issues can be a source of impatience with the humanities. It may begin to look as if its insights are always fleeting. As if nothing is ever settled, nothing is fixed. As if the best that can be hoped for is something akin to what Frost once provocatively declared to be the aim of a poetry: a momentary stay against confusion.[5]

---

5. Robert Frost, "The Figure a Poem Makes," in *Collected Poems of Robert Frost* (New York: Holt, Rinehart, and Winston, 1939).

The appropriate response to such worries is to not be overly defensive. It is to concede that Frost's declaration may have some relevance for the humanities, but only if "momentary" is taken as poetic hyperbole. The insights are transitory relative to the great sweep of time. Their shelf lives can be measured in decades, and in some cases centuries, but not for all times and all audiences. Except perhaps for a few sharply defined descriptive issues, there can be no notion of getting closer and closer to an intellectual stopping point. Nothing can permanently relieve future generations of needing to work on the same sorts of issues as grappled with by current and past generations. For these issues, there is no end to the story.

INTELLECTUAL PROGRESS

At the opposite of the spectrum from those who argue that the basic sciences are now so advanced that current theories going forward will not require anything more than tinkering are skeptics who maintain that there has been little or no progress at all. According to them, the history of science is mostly a history of errors, with later theories regularly overthrowing earlier ones in revolutions so complete that the earlier ones are dismissed as largely mistaken. This take on the history then becomes the basis for a pessimistic prediction, according to which currently favored theories will likewise be thoroughly discredited by future ones, which themselves will then be subject to yet further revolutions.[6]

---

6. Much of the inspiration for these pessimistic views derives from Thomas Kuhn's work on scientific revolutions, although he himself had more modulated views about progress in science. See Thomas Kuhn, *The Structure of Scientific Revolutions*, 3rd ed. (Chicago: University of Chicago Press, 1996).

This bleak assessment, however, is based on a reading of the history of modern science that is not defensible. There have been cases of wholesale debunking, the phlogiston theory of combustion being a celebrated example, but these are exceptions. In general, prior theories get corrected while having most of their elements incorporated into later theories, as opposed to being utterly discarded. And as the sciences have continued to develop, the pattern has been for fewer and fewer of their central claims to be completely abandoned.

Moreover, even when there are doubts, as there sometimes are, about some of the more exotic commitments of current theories (modern cosmology comes to mind), this does not affect the basic point. There is still a compelling story of progress to be told of increasing empirical adequacy over time,[7] with later theories able to predict ever wider ranges of observable phenomena, which in turn has led to an accelerating, and impossible to ignore, pace of technological advancement.

So, it is best not to deny the obvious. There has been progress in the sciences— indeed, an impressive amount of it. Not that the trajectory has had a continuous upward slope. There have periods of stagnation or even periods when understanding of an issue seemed to recede. This was what led Pierre Duhem to his metaphor that scientific progress is like a mounting tide, where underneath the back-and-forth movement of waves is an overall rise.[8] The tide metaphor is often apt, but it does not adequately capture the idea that progress has sometimes come in big jumps. But whatever the pattern, with enough time there generally has been improved understanding. Today's knowledge of astronomy, to take but one example, is

7. See Bas van Fraassen, *The Scientific Image* (Oxford: Clarendon Press, 1980).
8. Pierre Duhem, *The Aim and Structure of Physical Theory* (Princeton, NJ: Princeton University Press, 1954).

more complete and precise than that of Kepler's time; but by the same token, Kepler's theory of how the planets travel around the sun was an improvement over that of Copernicus, which was an advance over geocentric accounts. This is the history of astronomy to which virtually every contemporary astronomer subscribes, and what is true of astronomy is true also of the histories of most other scientific fields.

Progress in the humanities is sometimes contrasted unfavorably with the sciences, but the critiques typically assume that the criteria for marking progress are the same; but they are not. The issues are different and so are the insights being sought. As a result, the progress to be made in them is also different. Different in kind.

Recall some of the representative questions addressed by the humanities. How did political systems, religions, or intellectual assumptions come into being, and what are their important commonalities and differences? What economic, societal, and geographical factors, and which individuals and groups, influenced their development? And were those influences for better or worse? What roles have literature, music, art, and other cultural products played in individual lives and human societies? How have the features of these works differed over time and place, and what are successful and unsuccessful examples of such works? What is the nature of morality and justice—what claims do they make on us, and how have different societies and times interpreted these claims? For topics such as these, the aim cannot be to develop definitive treatments that would relieve future generations of the need for further inquiry. Nor is this an ideal to try to approach.

Progress in the sciences can be visualized as occurring on a vertical axis, with movement in an upward direction toward a collectively agreed upon endpoint. Not so for the humanities. Progress there comes more in the form of greater breadth, coherence, and precision, and with individual progress being highly prized even when it doesn't lead to a convergence of opinion.

Greater precision is typically achieved through the introduction of distinctions. In her work on the humanities, Helen Small talks of the importance of taking "pleasure in the specificity of the object of study and the specificity of the individual response."[9] Details matter, and because they matter, there is always room for more distinctions, which when made well result in accounts of enhanced clarity and depth. The path to greater breadth and coherence is to come to grips with issues in ways that connect them with other issues, both those within the field and those outside it. At minimum, views about various issues should not be in tension with one another; the higher standard is for them to positively reinforce one another, in which case the result is a more defensible whole. If an image is needed for this kind of progress, it might be visualized as occurring on a horizontal as opposed to a vertical axis, with additional distinctions increasing the density of plotted points along the axis and with additional links between issues increasing the overall spread of the plotted points.

But whatever the image, think of progress in the humanities by way of comparison with the development of a body of law over time and the role played by appellate judges in this development. Many of the cases coming before judges arise from a need to apply existing law to new circumstances. Sometimes it is just a novel combination of factors that raises new issues, but other times it is broad contextual changes that do so: different economic realities, new social practices, technological advances, and so on. Judges are expected to be fully familiar with the facts and context of the case, as well as with the history of relevant past rulings; but to arrive at a decision, they

9. Helen Small, *The Value of the Humanities* (Oxford: Oxford University Press, 2013).

often also need to reach beyond the law and draw upon ethical or political values. When doing so, they should make use of those they would also find acceptable outside the judicial contexts.[10] And then, before finalizing any decision, they should be prepared to articulate the bases of any disagreements between their prospective ruling and those made in similar cases. Their task is to fit all these elements— the new circumstances, the facts of the case at hand, the existing body of law, possible revisions or extensions of it, relevant extralegal values, the nature of any differences between their ruling and other rulings—into a package they are prepared to stand behind, one that further reflection won't cause them to amend. Their finding should in this sense be invulnerable at least to self-criticism.

It is "at least" because others may be highly critical of the decision. And even if the decision does not immediately provoke disagreements, it remains open to testing and revision as further new circumstances emerge. So, it is not as if the decision is expected to settle the issue for all time. Still, when all goes well, the result is a body of law of greater precision, clarity, breadth, and coherence. In other words, there is progress, or if one prefers, one can instead talk of "development." The term doesn't matter so much. What does matter is that the picture is not one of stasis.

Progress, or development, in the humanities can be conceived similarly, with humanities scholars playing a role analogous to that of judges. There are important differences, to be sure. Judges in most legal systems are in situations of forced decision making. Under certain circumstances, they can refuse to consider a case, but once accepted, there has to be a ruling. It can be on narrow grounds in an effort to constrain its applicability to other situations, but some

10. Ronald Dworkin, *Law's Empire* (Cambridge, MA: Harvard University Press, 1986); and Dworkin, *Justice for Hedgehogs*.

conclusion or another has to be reached. Moreover, once the decision is announced, it has the force of law. Neither of these situations has a counterpart in the humanities.

In other respects, however, there are striking analogies. Some are obvious. Just as judges must master the facts of their cases, humanities scholars must master the materials relevant to their issues, whether these are archival materials or texts or whatever. And just as judges have a responsibility to understand the rulings of current and past peers, and the bases of any disagreements with them, so too humanities scholars should be conversant with the views not only of their contemporaries but also of past scholars who have dealt with the same or similar topics. In the next section ("Intellectual Authority"), I discuss the related question of why it is that classic works in the humanities are more relevant to their current inquiries than classic works in the sciences are to theirs, but for now the point is that humanities scholars, unlike scientists, always have a reason to take an interest in the history of their fields that is not merely antiquarian.[11]

There are further parallels. Changing circumstances—economic, social, political, intellectual, or some other—can create a need for revised interpretations of existing law, and as such they are occasions for progress. So, too, in the humanities new circumstances often necessitate fresh looks at entrenched views and ignored issues, and are opportunities for progress. Moreover, some of the most far-reaching examples of these reassessments arise out of engagements with new scientific knowledge.

A case in point is evolutionary biology, which over last century or so has shown with increasing detail how the bodies and faculties of humans have been shaped by the same processes of natural

11. I owe Philip Pettit for making this observation about philosophy in particular. >

selection that shaped other animal and plant life. To many (but to be sure, not all), these insights now seems unexceptional, but they represent a profound shift from earlier eras that insisted on a sharp distinction between humans and other living things. They did so in large part by deemphasizing biological similarities between human life and other life and by fixating instead on nonbiological properties thought to single out humans from other life, such as having a soul or a faculty of reason. The implications of this shift are still being worked out in a wide variety of domains, and the humanities are no exception. It is one of the factors responsible for increased interest across the humanities in developing new insights about the similarities, differences, and appropriate relationships between humans and animals that are fully compatible with their shared evolutionary history.

In analogous ways, political and social developments are also occasions for reconsidering previously held views or taking up new issues. The movement for women's rights is one example, but a powerful one. It sparked political and social reforms, but in addition has led to major changes in the kinds of research undertaken in the humanities. Early on, these changes were primarily driven by, and most evident in, women's studies programs, but the effects are now pronounced across the entire sweep of the humanities.

It is the general dynamic that most needs emphasizing here, however. Coming to grips with cases in a manner consistent with new political, ethical, or social realities or with scientific and technological advances is a standard way that a body of law is developed and a kind of progress is made—a horizontal progress that carries no implications about getting closer to a final definitive resolution of the issues. In a like manner, changes outside the sphere of the humanities can prompt reevaluations of previously held views, this being a way that fields in the humanities can collectively progress.

If work in a field is revised to be compatible with current scientific knowledge in ways that much of the earlier work was not, this represents an advance, just as it does in the law. Similarly, just as the development of a body of law over time is in part a matter of keeping up with evolving ethical, political, or social standards, so too this can be the case in the humanities. If much of the previous work in the field was incompatible with an important ethical and political norm whereas most current work is compatible, this again is a mark of progress, even if it is progress that piggybacks on developments elsewhere.

Social, political, and ethical changes outside the sciences affect what issues are taken up by them as well, and can even modify how science is done. Think again of how guidelines for the ethical treatment of humans and animal subjects in experiments and clinical trials have changed over time. But as discussed earlier, although ethical, political, and social considerations can give direction to scientific inquiry and impose constraints on it, the goal is for them to then drop out and not influence the conclusions reached. In the humanities and the law, by contrast, the objective can be just the opposite—that of ensuring that the conclusions reached are compatible with evolving ethical, social, and political standards.

Ethical and political norms are often contested, of course, but not always to the same degree. In many regions of the world there has been impressive movement over time in the direction of greater acceptance of human rights, as well as greater acknowledgment that those rights not to be restricted to one race, gender, or nationality. To the extent that this movement is reflected internally in a country's body of law or a body of work in a humanities field, this is a basis for saying that it has advanced.

Even so, whenever issues are intertwined in major ways with ethical and political values, there is the possibility of controversy.

There is, accordingly, also plenty of room for controversy about whether changes prompted by such values have really been for the better. In legal systems, there are mechanisms for dealing with such disagreements. A judge's ruling is no less binding for being controversial. Not that it can never be reversed—it can be—but in the interim it has the force of law. But in the humanities, when there are controversies over evolving values and the new developments they stimulate, there is no mechanism for resolving them.

This can limit the amount and the pace of collective progress, and it is also associated with the greater emphasis on individual progress that is characteristic of the humanities. The major political, social, and intellectual changes that tend to trigger reassessments in the humanities are ones for which most scholars would in any event find it important to have their own views. So for them, there is often something not just professionally compelling but also intensely personal about these reassessments. It is a difficult and lengthy project for anyone to develop coherent views about issues linked to rapidly changing social, political, and intellectual conditions. Indeed, it is difficult and lengthy enough for a lifetime when the conditions are continually evolving, as they often are. But even in periods of stability, there remain plenty of occasions for such reevaluations. We are all social believers; the bulk of our opinions having been formed early in life, usually without much thought. Reflecting on which of these views we are willing to continue to stand by is never irrelevant. There is always a conversation to be had with one's own intellectual inheritance. For humanities scholars, however, there is more. There is more because, in addition to these personal elements, which are themselves germane to their work as scholars (I return to this point in a moment), they have a responsibility to take a stand. This is part of their job description as experts.

William James argued that everyone has intellectual obligations to try not only to believe truths but also to avoid errors. These obligations might look equivalent, but they are not. If the latter were the only concern, the right tactic would be the risk-averse one of accepting only that which is close to certain, even though this might mean missing out on likely truths. If the former were the only concern, the appropriate strategy would be to accept whatever is more likely to be true than not, even though doing so would increase the chances of falling into error. The challenge, says James, is to find an appropriate balance.[12]

For those who lack the necessary training and relevant information about an issue, the right balance is to refrain from making any judgment at all on their own. The situation is different for experts, however. All else being equal, they are expected to not straddle the fence on issues about which they have expertise. If they lack relevant information or training, they are to try to get it. This is not always immediately feasible, however, in which case they too can withhold coming to a conclusion, given that the situation of most experts, unlike judges, is not one of forced decision making. Still, their default responsibility is to do their best to get themselves eventually into a position where they are able to take a stand.

This can be challenging, and in the humanities it is made all the more so by the nature of the issues. Many have prescriptive elements, and in order to take a stand on them, scholars, like judges, need to appeal to values. An earlier example was of historians who are interested not only in accurately describing the events of the Battle of Waterloo but also in assessing the wisdom of Napoleon's decisions. The relevant norms for making such judgments are not specific to history, though. They are ones appropriate for evaluating

12. William James, *Essays in Pragmatism* (New York: Hafner, 1948).

military and political decisions in general. Historians wanting to appraise the choices made at Waterloo thus need to think hard about norms of military and political leadership and apply them to the circumstances faced by Napoleon. And, as is again the case with judges, the values they employ in reaching their conclusions should be ones they are willing to stand behind outside of their professional context. This is an aspect of the merger of the personal and the professional I referred to earlier.

The merging of personal and professional is also evident in the manner in which scholars influence their fields. They are no different from other advocates in wanting to have such influence. But because there is less of an expectation or demand for consensus in the humanities, their core responsibility is to make personal progress on their issues—that is, to develop accounts of greater precision, breadth, and coherence that they themselves are willing to stand behind, even if other experts disagree. Other experts, of course, have the same responsibility; they too, after considering rival views, may be prepared to stand behind their accounts. This can produce the look of a stalemate, but, as stated earlier, there is no point at which the dialogue has to end. When it comes to the kinds of issues the humanities deal with, the standard package offers no prospect of arriving at a stopping point where further inquiry, deliberation, and debate are out of place.

Besides, standoffs can have their good sides. They can force the disputants to reexamine seemingly obvious presuppositions, which in turn may lead to deeper insights. And of course, it is not as if anyone has a corner on the truth with respect to these issues. So, it never hurts to keep an open mind, even about those ideas that one feels confident about, and when the disagreements with one's own views are widespread, there are especially strong reasons to think again. My grandfather's salty advice to his grandsons was: "If everyone around you is telling you that your fly is open, you'd better look down."

There is likewise no shortage of circumstances in the sciences in which experts find that they cannot agree. Here, too, deadlocks can cause the disputants to reexamine the bases for their views, which in turn may lead to revisions and improvements. This being said, the desire to predict and control, as well as understand, the world creates more pressure to resolve deadlocks and arrive at a consensus— if not immediately, then at least over time. Moreover, the issues in the sciences are such that eventual agreement is ordinarily more practicable than in the humanities, even if the route to that agreement is long and difficult.

INTELLECTUAL AUTHORITY

Great works in the sciences become dated more quickly than those in the humanities. Kepler and Descartes were close contemporaries. Kepler was born in 1571 and died in 1630, while Descartes's dates were 1596 to 1650. Both made enormous contributions, Kepler to astronomy and Descartes to several fields but especially philosophy. Yet Kepler's most famous work, *New Astronomy,* is rarely a part of the training of current students in astronomy, while philosophy students are still expected to have a working familiarity with Descartes's *Meditations on First Philosophy.*

Why the difference? Because the kinds of progress to be made in the two fields are different. In philosophy generally, there cannot be progress on its issues in the direction of definitive accounts on which there is a general consensus, whereas in astronomy, there can be and has been such progress. Kepler's works are thus too dated to be of direct use to contemporary astronomers.

To be sure, Descartes also defended positions that are now regarded as dated. His view of the pineal gland as the location where the mind interacts with the body is a prime example, but his philosophical positions and the arguments he used to defend them still attract attention. This is not because contemporary philosophers are inclined to endorse them, however. What does account for the interest, then?

Intellectual systems, whether in the humanities, sciences, or any other domain, that are majestically ambitious can be enlightening, even when they are deeply flawed. They can be of interest for their overall argumentative strategies, as well as for particular points they make along the way; but they can also be instructive in the ways they fail. Descartes's system is of interest for all three reasons, but perhaps especially the last. It is often the analysis of where and how his system goes wrong that contemporary philosophers find most relevant in developing their own accounts. I give an illustration of this in the book's conclusion, "A Plea for Intellectual Humility," but for now the main point is that because it is not feasible to settle philosophy's core problems once and for all, the current significance of its classical works has to be measured differently from developments in the sciences. Contributions in philosophy are not to be evaluated in terms of whether they have been helpful in moving the field toward a consensus but, instead, assessed in terms of whether they can be of help in thinking about the issues with greater clarity, detail, breadth, and coherence. Close attention to the works of classical thinkers can be valuable in this way even when few if any contemporary thinkers agree with those views. I once gave a lecture to undergraduate philosophy students titled, "Why Descartes Is One of the Greatest Philosophers Who Ever Lived Despite Being Wrong About Almost Everything." The title was a gimmick, but behind it was this very point.

Classical texts in the sciences, by contrast, do not have as much relevance for current inquiries. At least not directly. They can be thought of as still mattering in the sense that their best insights have been absorbed into the body of collective knowledge that current inquirers continue to draw upon, Kepler's laws of planetary motion again are a case in point. The texts themselves are no longer pertinent; even when they still are assigned to students, the usual purpose is not so much to convey information as to be exemplars of scientific thinking.

This does not mean that Kepler's texts are not of great contemporary interest, however. They are, but the insights to be found in them are now largely about the history of ideas, which is a traditional concern of the humanities. Historians and philosophers of science still study Kepler's *New Astronomy* because it is a window into understanding the scientific revolution. Similarly, Harvey's writings on the circulatory system remain fascinating because they are revelatory about the roots of contemporary medicine. It may sound paradoxical, but these works are now often best read as humanities texts.

Influence is exercised differently in the humanities and arts than it is in the sciences. The influence can continue to be direct over long stretches of time in the sense that the vehicles of influence can be the preserved works themselves. This is palpably true of the arts— Shakespeare's plays are still studied and performed, Michelangelo's sculptures are still analyzed, and Rembrandt's self-portraits are still debated—but it is also the case in the humanities. The works of Thucydides, Gibbon, Carlyle, and de Tocqueville are still taken seriously by historians and their students, as are those of Aristotle, Descartes, Hume, Locke, and Kant by current philosophers.

Although classic works in the humanities are more relevant to its current inquiries than those in the sciences are to theirs, reliance on expert authority plays a less central role in the humanities than in the sciences. These observations might appear to be in tension, but they are not. Two further observations explain why. The first is that the continuing relevance of great historical figures in the humanities is not a matter of deference to their authority. (More on this shortly.) The second is that although in the sciences there is extensive reliance on authority, the relevant authorities are contemporary specialists, not the great figures of the past.

A familiar adage is that contemporary scientists stand upon the shoulders of giants. The image may be hackneyed. It is also imperfect, since it fails to capture the importance of not just relying on the findings of one's predecessors but also on correcting their mistakes. The image is nonetheless compelling. Indeed, doubly so, since it manages to convey not only how scientists make use of the stock of knowledge built up by previous generations but also how they do so without needing to have face-to-face contact with them. They employ their results, but they do not have to engage them directly. They instead stand on their shoulders.

This image might seem to verge on disrespectful, as if later scientists were saying to earlier ones, "Okay, you did your thing, but now your only significance is to serve as our step stools." But science is a collective and temporally extended enterprise, and within it, the impersonal quality of its attitudes toward fellow inquirers, past and present, is a virtue, not a problem. With respect to past experts, the system allows current inquirers to make use of their best findings—the ones that have withstood the test of time and hence are preserved in the collective knowledge of the field while by and large ignoring that which is outdated. With respect to contemporary experts, the system is designed to allow inquirers to trust the findings of other inquirers, even those in subfields so specialized that only they are in a position to provide firsthand defenses of the findings. Their findings are nonetheless available to the larger scientific community.

Deference to the expertise of specialists is not automatic and it is not irrevocable. There are always decisions to be made about whom to trust, when to trust, and how much to trust. The overall system, however, has features that make it reasonable to have presumptive confidence in the findings of other inquirers. One of these features is its public character. The conclusions of even the most esteemed authorities are open to scrutiny. Even they must make the data they collect available to others, and even they must formulate their hypotheses so that others can test them. Still, in the real world of science, even when other scientists have the necessary expertise to reconfirm hypotheses, there are limits on how much time and effort they should spend doing so. After all, one of the most important benefits of the division of intellectual labor is that it frees inquirers to work on addressing their own specialized issues. Besides, if anomalies eventually begin to show up in their own work, they can always go back and reexamine the results of others they have relied upon.

Prima facie trust in the opinions of others, even those whom we do not know personally, permeates all corners of our lives; but within the practice of science, it has an especially central and organized role. The trust extends beyond other investigators to the technicians, graduate students, and post-docs who do much of the everyday work in laboratories. It extends also to those who build advanced equipment upon which many sciences rely—imagers, accelerators, bubble chambers, scanning tunneling microscopes, and the like. While some investigators may understand the engineering details of their equipment, many do not; nevertheless, they can and do make reasonable use of it. Their trust is in the expertise of those who designed and built it, and in other investigators who have had successful experiences using it.

There are delicate questions about how best to preserve the long-term integrity of a system that relies extensively on the views of strangers and the information generated by them, as well as questions about how best to balance the need for such trust against the danger that an overreliance on others might impede innovation.[13] For purposes here, however, the key point is that, with its collective goals, science has reliance on expert authority built into its core. Not blind reliance; there are limits. But because the practices are designed to surface inaccuracies, as well as dishonesty, they engender a presumption of trust. Investigators regularly rely on the findings of specialists whom they do not know, and they can reasonably do so even when they would be unable to mount an adequate defense of the findings on their own.

In the humanities, by contrast, there is more emphasis on intellectual self-reliance. There is scant room for deference to the great historical figures, but the same is true for leading contemporary scholars. For the most part, dependence on their authority is also to be avoided.

Indeed, self-reliance has been a major feature of Western intellectual tradition since the European Enlightenment. As otherwise different as the philosophies of Locke and Emerson were, making up one's own mind about consequential issues was at the center of both. In placing so much stress on this, they may have underestimated the extent to which our views cannot help but be shaped by the people around us and by our historical context, and hence they may not have fully appreciated how difficult genuine intellectual independence can be. Even so, the ethos of intellectual self-reliance these figures helped to create continues to be influential, including in the humanities.

---

13. For a thorough treatment of these issues, see Philip Kitcher, *The Advancement of Science* (Oxford: Oxford University Press, 1993).

In the societies that were most directly influenced by the European Enlightenment, suspicions about deference to authority tend to get expressed most fervently at the individual level. The autonomy most treasured is that of an individual resisting the authority of other individuals or groups. There are other societies, however, where issues of autonomy, especially those related to core questions of culture, ethics, and politics, are played out more at the level of society as a whole, the dominant concern being that of resisting the hegemony of one's own society by more powerful ones. Within these latter societies, though, the prevailing climate may well be one of deference to political or religious authorities. When this is so, it can be difficult for the humanities to flourish, since their role may be restricted to that of preserving cultural traditions, retelling received histories, and reinforcing desired ethical and political norms, all with the help of classic texts regarded as authoritative. The humanities thrive in environments where their influence is primarily Socratic, as opposed to deference to authority.

As remarked earlier, there is no sharp line dividing the two. They often work in combination with another, a mixture of deference and firsthand understanding that leads one to agree with the views of another. More generally, for there to be Socratic influence, the receiving party needs to be open to persuasion, which requires some degree of recognition that the other is in a guiding position on the issue, whether because of training, information, or some other factor. Still, when all is said and done, there is a difference between being persuaded and deferring, and it is an important one. It is the difference between making up one's own mind about something and taking someone else's word for it.

Even in the humanities, there are circumstances in which accepting claims on the basis of authority is not at all out of place, but when and where this is the case is itself telling. The contexts are generally ones in which the issues are both wholly descriptive and highly indexical, and where consequently the humanities, like the sciences, can readily profit from a division of intellectual labor. These are also issues, unlike others in the humanities, for which it is sometimes possible to arrive at something approaching a definitive account. Because there can be definitive accounts, there can also be definitive authorities.

The examples given earlier were the details of a particular event (its time, location, participants, etc.) or the provenance of a painting or manuscript, but there are plenty of other examples of sharply defined descriptive issues. David Levering Lewis, the biographer of W. E. B. DuBois, devoted ten years to producing a massive two-volume biography of DuBois. So, it is to be expected that when other historians are working on issues that involve DuBois, they defer to Lewis on the details of DuBois's education, travels, acquaintances, publicly expressed opinions, and personal life.[14] Deference on these issues is reasonable because of Lewis's standing as a historian and his track record for careful scholarship. Plus, it allows other scholars to concentrate on answering their own questions. All this is closely analogous to the situation in the sciences.

Lewis also defends various evaluative claims about DuBois, both general ones about his being one of the twentieth century's most important intellectuals and more specific ones about the defensibility of his political views.[15] Claims of this sort rely on value judgments about what constitutes significant intellectual contributions and what are reasonable grounds for political views. They also

14. David Levering Lewis, *W.E.B. DuBois, 1868–1919: Biography of a Race* (New York: Henry Holt, 1993); and David Levering Lewis, *W.E.B. DuBois: The Fight for Equality and the American Century, 1919-1963* (New York: Henry Holt, 2000).

15. See especially chapter 15, "Exeunt," in Lewis, *W.E.B. DuBois: The Fight for Equality and the American Century*.

have a wide scope, being concerned not just with the life of DuBois or even American history but instead with the entire sweep of the twentieth century. Lewis provides impressive support for his conclusions, but it is no insult to his standing as a historian that other historians should be reluctant to defer to his authority here. With respect to these claims, the model should be Socratic persuasion, not authority.

It is not unusual for ordinary people in their everyday lives to exhibit a similar wariness about deferring to others on value-laden issues. To be sure, there are those whose standing practice is to defer to the authorities they recognize, but many people are reluctant to simply borrow moral, political, or aesthetic opinions from others. Opening themselves up to persuasion is a different matter. In the case of aesthetic issues, for example, they may actively seek the views of expert critics because doing so will help make them more discerning, and thus will put them in a better position to arrive at and defend their own nuanced judgments about novels, films, paintings, architectural designs, or whatever else is in question.

Scholars in the humanities should be even more wary of deference. With the exception of those issues that are descriptive and highly indexical, there is not much space in the humanities for the practice of borrowing opinions, not even from other experts. The primary model of influence should instead be Socratic. This is so for a number of interconnected reasons: (1) the issues are commonly ones that require inquirers to make prescriptive judgments; (2) they frequently require inquirers to develop interpretations of the motivations and points of view of the individuals or groups under study, where these interpretations are shaped to some extent by the inquirer's own perspective; (3) the issues often are not easy to break down into sharply defined subissues; and (4) even when a breakdown is possible, the insights about the subissues are not likely to constitute a step in the direction of a definitive, collective resolution of the larger issue.

Socratic influence is also present throughout the sciences. It is centrally important, for example, in the training of advanced students, since the aim of such training is to put the students into a position whereby they are capable of formulating their own research agendas. In addition, although there is as wide a range of motivations for engaging in scientific inquiry as there are for any other kind of activity, many scientists are driven by personal curiosity. They have a desire to acquire as much firsthand understanding as possible of the phenomena that interest them. This makes them open and even eager to being tutored by others, but they prefer not to simply rely on the authority of anyone else. They ideally would like to be able to fully defend any conclusions they accept, even though in practice there are limits on how much of their knowledge meets this criterion, and even though science is a system organized to expand the collective stock of knowledge that investigators can reasonably employ when they are not able to give firsthand defenses of it.

So, the thesis here, once again, has to be understood as one of relative emphasis. In the sciences, reliance on the opinions of experts, and more specifically on opinions one is not in a position to defend oneself, has a larger and more defining role than it can properly have in the humanities, where the default aims are insights that are one's own, to the degree possible. The goal is thus similar to what John Locke maintained was always and everywhere the aim of inquiry:

> For, I think, we may as rationally hope to see with other Mens Eyes, as to know by other Mens Understandings. So much as we our selves consider and comprehend of Truth and Reason,

so much we possess of real and true Knowledge. The floating of other Mens Opinions in our brains makes us not one jot the more knowing, though they happen to be true. What in them was science, is in us but Opiniatretry, whilst we give up our Assent only to reverend names, and do not, as they did, employ our own Reason to *understand* those *Truths*, which gave them reputation. . . . In the Sciences, every one has so much, as he really knows and comprehends: What he believes only, and takes upon trust, are but shreds; which however well in the whole piece, make no considerable addition to his stock, who gathers them. Such borrowed Wealth, like Fairy-money, though it were Gold in the hand from he received it, will be but Leaves and Dust when it comes to use.[16]

"Science" in this passage has a pre-scientific revolution meaning that is roughly equivalent to knowledge generally. Locke is thus expressing his contempt for any reliance at all on intellectual authority. He is making an appeal for people to make full use of their own faculties in thinking through issues for themselves.

Locke's egalitarianism, individualism, and optimism are all on vivid display here. His exhortation is for even ordinary people (his egalitarianism) to rely on their own judgment and reason (individualism); and his reassuring claim is that if they are careful about gathering evidence and conforming to their opinions to this evidence, the result will be "real and true knowledge" (optimism). These are characteristics that make Locke one of the paradigmatic figures of the European Enlightenment. They also combine to make him utterly distrustful of intellectual authority. His view was that there

16. John Locke, An *Essay Concerning Human Understanding,* ed. Peter Nidditch (Oxford: Clarendon Press, 1975), 101.

is always something substandard in taking someone else's word for the truth of a claim. He had no objection to Socratic influence, because in such cases one comes to understand for one's self why the claim in question is true, but when one relies on the intellectual authority of others, the resulting belief is no more than "the floating of other Mens Opinions in our brains." It is "borrowed wealth, like Fairy-money."

Locke's heady mixture of egalitarianism, individualism, and optimism can no longer be defended in the unrestricted way he intended—that is, as the appropriate epistemology for all people, all situations, and all domains. He was too skeptical of the practice of making use of the opinions of others, underappreciative of how massive our dependence on the opinions of others is, insufficiently aware about what a potentially powerful tool deference to the authority of experts can be in certain domains, and overly dismissive of the everyday demands on ordinary people, which leave them limited time for independent inquiry and reflection.

This being said, the Lockean model is by and large an appropriate epistemology for the humanities. Here, the aim, again with the exception of issues that are thoroughly descriptive and narrowly indexical, should be for individual scholars to minimize the reliance on the opinions of others "floating in their brains," and should instead to the extent possible arrive at conclusions they are able to defend on their own without appeals to the authority of others.

SIMPLICITY AND COMPLEXITY

One of the working hypotheses of the sciences is that the laws of nature are simple. So, all else being equal, the fewer the assumptions and postulates, the better the theory.

Here is what Galileo said about simplicity: "Nature does not multiply things unnecessarily; that she makes use of the easiest and simplest means for producing her effects; that she does nothing in vain, and the like."[17] Likewise, at the beginning of Book III of *Principia Mathematica*, Newton lists simplicity among his principal rules and goes on to observe: "Nature is pleased with simplicity, and affects not the pomp of superfluous causes."[18] In the twentieth century, Albert Einstein made the point in this way: "Our experience hitherto justifies us in trusting that nature is the realization of the simplest that is mathematically possible."[19]

The case that Galileo, Newton, and Einstein were making for simplicity was not merely aesthetic or pragmatic. Simpler theories may be more beautiful and easier to use, but their claim was that complexity is a sign that a theory does not have things quite right. The preference for simpler theories is in service to the search for truth.

This is not an unconditional preference. There are plenty of contexts in which the sciences demand an appreciation of complexity. Understanding and being able to predict the behavior of systems, for example, involves knowing the details of how its components interact. The human body is a case in point, which is why medical interventions should be grounded in a holistic understanding of how the body's parts and processes are interrelated. The same is true of interventions in ecological systems. Even so, an appreciation of the complexity of a system is compatible with the presumption that simple and universal (or near universal)

17. Galileo, *Dialogue Concerning the Chief Two World Systems* (Berkeley: University of California Press, 9162), 397.
18. Isaac Newton, *Principia Mathematica* (Cambridge, MA: Harvard University Press, 1972), 398.
19. Albert Einstein, *On the Method of Theoretical Physics* (Oxford: Clarendon Press, 1954), 183

processes are governing the interactions of its parts. Thinks of efforts to understand the bases of intricate systems in the human brain and body in terms of the humble cellular processes that occur even in yeast.[20]

In the humanities, by contrast, there should not be and normally is not as strong al partiality for simplicity. On the contrary, the presumptive attitude should be one of wariness. Simplicity can be a warning flag that important details are getting ignored or, worse, that an all-encompassing ideology is at work. A taste for some complexity should be the norm.

An apparent exception is philosophy. In the section "Philosophy, the Humanities, the Sciences" (chapter 4), I discuss philosophy's relationships with the sciences and the humanities, along with the closely related issue of the value it places on simplicity. For the moment, however, put it to one side. Throughout most of the rest of the humanities, there is a characteristic respect for complexity and a corresponding guardedness about simplicity.

These attitudes are by-products of the issues being indexical and intertwined with the conscious states and points of view of humans, which themselves are inherently complex. Not that complexity is to be valued for its own sake, either. Details matter in the humanities, but to paraphrase Tennyson, detail piled upon detail would still be all too little. There are countless truths associated with every situation, but many are of little significance. An excess of specifics can even be an obstacle, making it more difficult to pick out important features. Recall the Jorge Luis Borges story of a kingdom where people became so obsessed with exactness in cartography that only

---

20. See, for example, a summary of the research being done in the laboratory of Nobel laureate Randy Schekman, at http://mcb.berkeley.edu/labs/schekman/index.html.

with a map of the kingdom with a scale of one-to-one would satisfy them. Accuracy is one thing; numbing detail is another.

So, even in the humanities, culling and simplifying are necessary. The search is for insights that are at the right level of detail to be helpful in understanding the subject matter at hand. In addition, it is all to the better when the insights have features also useful in understanding comparable phenomena elsewhere. But there are limits on how far they can be extended. To return to the example used earlier, insights about the social and political conditions in Paris at the time of the French Revolution are unlikely to be of major assistance in understanding early Inuit society.

Still, perhaps the single most important point to keep in mind when it comes to issues involving humans and human societies is that there is no uniquely best way of addressing them. It is often counterproductive to keep pressing for greater generality and simplicity, but not always. If one assumes an Olympian viewpoint about the approaches human inquirers take in seeking insights about their fellow humans, one sees that they can be placed into two broad categories. There are inquiries that are primarily focused on uncovering similarities and others that emphasize differences. This divide, in turn, corresponds roughly with the divide between the studies of humans one finds in the sciences and those in the humanities.

The sciences tell us that humans are extremely alike physically. We now know that there is an almost startlingly small amount of genetic diversity among humans compared with other mammalian species. We also know that there are striking genetic overlaps between humans and other living things. The similarities, moreover, are not limited to apes, chimps, and other mammals. Approximately three-fourths of the known human disease genes have recognizable matches in the genetic code of fruit flies.

These matches provide an exceptionally fertile ground for research. At virtually every major university, there are investigators working on the genetics of nonhuman life forms in hopes that this will lead to a better understanding of like processes in humans. These projects follow the familiar scientific pattern of assimilation and simplification. "All life is one" is the working aphorism. The same ingredients (DNA, RNA, proteins, and carbohydrates) form the basis of all known life, and the basic processes involving these ingredients are found not only in humans but also in fruit flies, worms, and yeast. Applying the knowledge, once again, is a different matter. Here, the differences across species, as well as differences within a single species, matter. An example is personalized medicine, where each person's unique variation of the human genome is used to custom-design treatments for curing disease and protocols for preventing it.

But it is not just for purposes of application that these differences are of interest. We humans tend to be just plainly curious about them, and we are especially curious about the differences among ourselves. This is not true of every one of us, of course, but a sign of our collective preoccupation with these differences is that we make far finer distinctions about one another than we do about anything else. There are detailed discriminations about our capacities, emotions, personalities, and backgrounds, but also about our physical features, environments, languages, and beliefs. And this is only the beginning. We make distinctions of gender, ethnicity, nationality, religious background, and age; and there seems to be almost inexhaustible interest in identifying social, cultural, economic, and other differences correlated with these categories. Individuals are also grouped by economic class, occupation, education, sexual orientation, and marital status; again, there is great interest in finding dissimilarities across these groups. There are more local groupings as well: the people who live in this neighborhood rather than that one, or who attended this school rather than some other. The list goes on and on. The availability of so many distinctions and the zeal with which they are deployed may sometimes make it appear as if people are enormously different from one another. But any careful look reveals this to be an exaggeration. Humans are remarkably similar.

Why, then, do our differences so intrigue us? Perhaps because a mastery of them helps us to navigate the intricacies of social relations. But whatever the explanation, it is with these discriminations that the humanities (and the arts) come into their own. The pattern in the sciences is to assimilate seemingly disparate phenomena in an effort to find generalizations that apply ever more widely. The pattern in the humanities is to look for ways of distinguishing even seemingly similar phenomena in an effort to reveal hitherto unnoticed complexities.

As always, these are tendencies. I have discussed how the emphasis on reducing indexicality in the sciences varies from field to field, and I have also made reference to there being a range of views in the humanities about how broadly to cast the net in the search for understanding. There are historians who focus on specific people, groups, and events, others who examine big political ideas and pervasive economic trends, and still others who look for long-term factors such as climate. Still, the overall propensities of the sciences and the humanities are poles apart. Assimilation and simplification on the one hand; diversification and complication on the other. Each has its place. There is potentially enormous power in simplicity and potentially great richness in complexity.

INVOLVEMENT WITH MENTALITY

The paradigmatic issues of the humanities arise because there are creatures with mental states. They are all involved in one way or another with aspects of mentality.

I use "mentality" as an umbrella term to cover the full range of states and processes that can be said to be conscious. Included are experiences with a distinct sensory feel, such as those associated with seeing a certain shade of red, hearing a bell ring, feeling a pinprick, tasting something salty, and smelling coffee. Feelings of hunger, thirst, coldness, and the like are also included, as are beliefs, desires, intentions, memories, and emotions. So is what Ned Block has called "access consciousness": if a state contains information that is available for use and guidance by a creature, it can be said to be conscious in this expansive sense, even if it is not associated with a distinct sensory feel and the creature is not currently aware of it.[21] In addition, there is a general "what it is like to be" sense, which refers to the way the world is experienced by a conscious creature.

Whereas the humanities focus almost exclusively on phenomena that involve mentality, the sciences for the most part do not. There are notable exceptions, of course. Perception, learning, memory, and emotions, to name a few, are all extremely active areas of scientific research. Then again, it is only a small fraction of living organisms that have conscious states, and living organisms are only a small fraction of everything there is. So, it is a tiny percentage of the issues of the sciences that are concerned with mentality, whereas virtually all issues in the humanities are. As importantly, when the

---

21. Ned Block, "On a Confusion About the Function of Consciousness," *Behavioral and Brain Sciences* 18 (1995): 227–247.

sciences do investigate mental phenomena, they do so in their own characteristic way.

The only conscious creatures currently available for the sciences to study are those that came into existence on a specific planet at a specific time in the relatively recent past and that at some unknown future time will pass out of existence. So, the insights being sought have an indexical cast. Still, as discussed earlier, the aim is to develop these insights in terms of processes and standing conditions not limited to Earth or to a particular time period. This along with the related pressure to minimize perspectival elements produces a preference for accounts that are based as much as possible on information from outside the sphere of what is inflected with consciousness and perspective—information for example, about the neurophysiological conditions associated with the mental phenomena in question.

This is not to say that there are not plenty of projects in the sciences that investigate mental phenomena while remaining at the level of the mental. It is standard for social psychologists and cognitive scientists to collect, or generate through experiments, data about the mental attitudes and processes of a set of subjects, and then to use these data to support conclusions, often statistical in nature, about related mental phenomena in the wider population. Still, the quantity and quality of this work notwithstanding, there is a high premium on discoveries about conscious phenomena that make little or no use of information itself inflected with mentality.

This has the effect of pushing inquiries in the direction of certain problems and away from others. There is a push, in particular, toward questions of origin and engineering. How did conscious phenomena come to be in the first place? How did they arise from nonconscious states and processes? What physical, biological, and computational properties are necessary for something to have conscious states at all, and what specific physical, biological, and computational properties are associated with particular conscious states and processes?

These are questions about mentality that the methods of the sciences are well positioned to address. They are ones for which there is a chance of answering in non-indexical and non-perspectival ways. The ultimate aim is to develop insights about the origins of consciousness and the kinds of organisms that can have conscious states from information about physical, biological, and computational processes that are not necessarily peculiar to humans or even living things on Earth. This is a formidable project, but then again, so is that of understanding gravity.

To some, however, the project has seemed not just difficult but also ill conceived. It is ill conceived, they say, because phenomena exhibiting mentality are so utterly distinctive. One way of dramatizing what is at stake is to consider whether it might be possible someday to fabricate out of chemical elements something that is alive and conscious, the assumption being that one understands what one can build from scratch. Imagine, as a gold standard for such work, a future in which science and engineering have advanced to the point where they are capable of creating "androids," to borrow a term from science fiction, which not only look like humans on the outside but also are able to mimic human behavior and capacities in every way.

There are those who maintain that these androids, despite their sophistication, would not be conscious beings with mental states. Others are not so sure. They wonder what reasons there would be for thinking that our fellow humans have conscious states while denying that these androids do. After all, by hypothesis, they mirror human behavior and capacities in every possible way, including verbal behavior and the diverse means humans have of monitoring their own internal states. Would a refusal to attribute conscious states to them be anything more than a human-centric bias?

There is now a large literature debating this question.[22] Lurking at the bottom of these debates is the gnarly metaphysical issue mentioned earlier. Are all the forms of consciousness and all the diverse expressions of consciousness found in animals, humans, and human societies the complicated effects of physical and biological processes, acting in accordance with fundamental laws?

But to repeat to what I said earlier, this is not my question. The question I am addressing arises whatever one thinks about the metaphysics of consciousness. Assume that all consciousness-related phenomena found in humans and human societies are supercomplex consequences of physical and biological processes, and assume as well that the sciences eventually will be able to provide minimally indexical and minimally perspectival explanations of the origins and engineering of conscious states. Even granting this, there is still a question as to whether these are the only kinds of insights about phenomena exhibiting mentality worth having. The answer is no.

The array of such phenomena is vast, and so is the knowledge we would like to have about them. We want whatever insights can be derived from information about chemical, biological, and computational processes in human brains, but we are also interested in those that are reflective of what it is like to be human and, when the phenomena in question involve specific individuals or groups, what it is like to be them.

---

22. For a sampling of this literature, see David Chalmers, "Facing Up to the Problem of Consciousness," *Journal of Consciousness Studies* 2 (1995): 200–219; Daniel Dennett, *Intuition Pumps and Other Tools for Thinking* (New York: W.W. Norton, 2013), especially chapter 7; Colin McGinn, *The Problem of Consciousness* (Oxford: Basil Blackwell, 1991); and Thomas Nagel, *Mind and Cosmos* (Oxford: Oxford University Press, 2013).

Consider some of the earlier-cited examples of projects in the humanities: descriptions of the Battle of Waterloo, along with evaluations of the wisdom of Napoleon's decisions leading up to and during the battle; depictions of masculinity and femininity in English and French romances of the late Middle Ages; accounts of the efforts to curb the polio epidemic in the mid-twentieth century; assessments of the social and political impacts of the life and works of W. E. B. DuBois; investigations of how the modernist movement influenced European and American architecture, art, and literature; and explications of the place of Mozart's operas within the history of opera and the society of eighteenth-century Europe.

All these projects are occupied with phenomena deeply entangled with the mentalities characteristic of humans; and the scholars seeking insights about them do so by developing portrayals, explanations, and analyses that make reference to the background beliefs, experiences, values, purposes, and other consciousness-inflected features of the people, societies, or times under investigation. The portrayals consist of detailed descriptions of the phenomena under study, including their similarities and dissimilarities with other consciousness-saturated phenomena. The explanations cite important "difference makers" in the dense network of factors leading to the occurrence of the phenomena, where these difference makers include ones that themselves display mentality.[23] The analyses articulate the structure and composition of the phenomena that exhibit mentality.

Portrayals, explanations, and analyses overlap and complement one another. Any particular account is likely to have elements of all three. David Oshinsky's history of efforts to fight the polio epidemic

---

23. For details on this way of thinking of explanations, see Michael Strevens, *Depth: An Account of Scientific Explanation* (Cambridge, MA: Harvard University Press, 2008).

has analyses of the strategies that rival scientists thought best for developing a vaccine, but it also proposes explanations of how public health measures helped (or in some cases failed to help) control the spread of the disease, and it contains portrayals of the personal competition, jealousies, and even public backbiting that went on between lead investigators.[24]

The crucial point for present purposes, however, is that in developing their accounts, scholars in the humanities need not feel pressured to rely exclusively on information from outside the sphere of the mental. They can be comfortable with their accounts being heavily dependent on considerations steeped in mentality. Moreover, this is not simply a convenience; it is indispensable insofar as some of the knowledge we want about people, their societies, and the forms of mentality they exhibit requires having a sense of how the people in question experienced their physical and social environments and how their experiences affected their behavior.

Let's return to the question posed in chapter 2 of what it is like to be a bat in a bat-like environment. A fully satisfying answer to this question would involve understanding what it is to experience the world when echolocation is added to vision, hearing, smell, touch, and taste. It would also include an appreciation of the holistic sense of the world that arises from the sensory faculties of bats interacting with their own bodies and the environments in which they operate, as well as the complex ways in which these interactions influence their behavior. Attempting to answer the question entirely from the "outside," without trying to take into account how bat environments seem from a bat's perspective, inevitably leaves out part of what is of interest.

24. David Oshinsky, *Polio: An American Story* (Oxford: Oxford University Press, 2006).

This is not just a point about bats, however. It applies also to other conscious creatures, most notably humans. There are insights to be had about their consciousness and lives that cannot be captured apart from a sense of how the world as experienced seems to them, the details of their world as thus experienced, and the ways in which these experiences intermingle with behavior, both individual and social. Investigative approaches that minimize indexicality and perspectivality are not well suited to produce insights of this sort.

Just the opposite approach is called for. For these issues, human inquirers should take advantage of their distinctive perspectival and indexical resources. They can extrapolate from their own case, drawing upon their own experiences and histories. They have firsthand understanding of what it is like to be a human living in a human-like environment. They need to make use of this knowledge. It is the basis they can use for making inferences about the mentality, lives, and behavior of other humans.

It is also the basis for them to use, although admittedly a shakier one, when trying to understand the mentality of other species. The sciences can be of assistance in these efforts. Information about how the perceptual faculties of the creatures being studied differ from those of humans is especially important—for example, that bats use echolocation, or some bird species have tetrachromatic vision, or octopuses have gustatory capacities in their tentacles. With such information in hand and observations about the behavior of these creatures, human inquirers can draw upon their firsthand knowledge of the ways in which human experiences and behavior tend to be interconnected to try to make inferences about the experiential takes that these nonhuman creatures have on their environments and the ways in which these experiences permeate their lives and behavior.

It is an understatement that these are not easy inferences to make. The differences among species are not trifling, but there are strategies that can help bridge the gap. Immersion of the sort practiced by anthropologists when studying human cultures, which involves observations of the subjects in their own environments over extended stretches of time, is especially useful, as Jane Goodall's studies of chimpanzees, Temple Grandin's work with livestock, and the research of many other ethologists have demonstrated. Even so, there are limits. The limits, moreover, are not just of scientific inquiry but, rather, of human inquiry in general.

With our fellow humans, however, there are extensive similarities for human inquirers to exploit. We have similar bodies, similar perceptual and cognitive faculties, and live in relatively similar environments. In our everyday lives, we constantly rely on our likenesses to make judgments about the mental states of those around us. Indeed, these judgments about one another permeate pretty much everything in our societies, from our politics and economics to our cultures and games.

There are different accounts of exactly how we go about deploying our similarities to reach conclusions about the mental states of each other. One view is that we do so with the aid of an elementary psychological theory, which we see applies in our own case and we then extend to others. Another is that we deploy some kind of rationality postulate, which we again observe is operative in ourselves and assume is likewise operative in others. Still another way is that we simulate what our own reactions would be were we to be in the situation of the other.[25] There are combinations of these

25. See Alvin Goldman, *Simulating Minds: The Philosophy, Psychology, and Neuroscience of Mindreading* (Oxford: Oxford University Press, 2008); and Shaun Nichols and Stephen Stich, *Mindreading: An Integrated Account of Pretense, Self-Awareness, and Understanding of Other Minds* (Oxford: Oxford University Press, 2003).

proposals as well, but they all acknowledge that even with fellow humans, there are significant obstacles to understanding, and perhaps even limitations on how fully we can comprehend them.

The obstacles are all the more challenging when the individuals of interest to us are distant in time, place, or culture. Still, with fellow humans, one's own case provides an entry into their subjective worlds. It is only an entry, however. To understand others, it is necessary to rely on one's own experiences and own history, but this always carries with it a risk of provincialism. Grasping the points of view of others, especially those in social environments unfamiliar to us, requires an effort to get beyond oneself and one's context in order to see others and their situations through their points of view. One has to start with one's own case, but this is not the final resting spot.

Difficult as the search for understanding of our fellow humans can be, the obstacles would be of a different order if we did not have roughly the same perceptual and cognitive equipment and did not live in broadly comparable physical and social environments. Imagine once again highly intelligent creatures elsewhere in the universe, with bodies, faculties, and ways of living sharply distinct from those of humans, trying to understand human consciousness, lives, and societal practices. Their challenges would be analogous to the ones we encounter in trying to understand bats and octopuses. In contrast, when the subjects of study are our fellow humans, we have built-in advantages that usually make it possible with enough time and effort to arrive at some measure of understanding, even of those who are far removed from us. The pathways for doing so, however, are ones that do not resist the indexical and perspectival; rather, they embrace them, which is just what the humanities do.

They are not alone. The arts embrace them as well. As I will be discussing in the section "Stories as Sources of Insight" in chapter 4, one of the most powerful tools the arts have for illuminating the points of views of others is the telling of stories, which themselves typically are both highly indexical and perspectival. In addition, as mentioned earlier, the fields of cognitive psychology and social psychology are rarely concerned with developing accounts of conscious phenomena wholly in terms of states and processes that do not exhibit mentality. The same is true of the social sciences more generally. I return to them and their position between the natural sciences and the humanities in "A Quick Look at the Social Sciences" (chapter 4), but for now the point is simply that humanities disciplines are not the only ones generating insights about phenomena associated with human consciousness from materials that are themselves inflected with mentality.

Whatever challenges there are in portraying, explaining, and analyzing consciousness-related phenomena in individual humans, they are multiplied when trying to understand social situations. In even the simplest of these situations—for example, those involving the relationship between only two individuals—the complexity explodes. The pair's relationship cannot be fully appreciated without understanding their points of view, which are packed with background information about the context. Moreover, the context is constantly changing. Their takes on each other's point of view are likewise continuously shifting. The first comes to an opinion about the second's actions or motives; the second recognizes that the first has this opinion, which changes the second's view of the first. The first then becomes aware of this shift, which in turn alters the first's view about the second, and so on.

The resulting density is such that individuals are often perplexed by the relationships in which they themselves are parties. External observers enjoy a distance that may allow them to discern more clearly overall patterns in the relationship, and they also may have the advantage of impartiality, but they are not as immersed in the details of the relationship as the participants themselves, and this can be an impediment to understanding.

For those outside the home culture, the impediments are all the greater. Background information that the agents themselves take for granted is so specific and nuanced that there are limits on to how completely those from other societies can absorb it. The outsiders can educate themselves, but again there are constraints. It is a commonplace that training in a culture is best done by living in it, but this is not feasible when the culture is spatially or temporally distant.

For instance, understanding Alexander Hamilton and his life would be easier for us if we had witnessed the Revolutionary War and the early years of the United States, and hence we had seen, heard, and experienced what Hamilton himself saw, heard, and experienced. Time travel is not an option, though. So, for us there is no close analogue of the immersion techniques used by cultural anthropologists to study unfamiliar cultures. We can comfort ourselves a little by the thought that the intricacies of Hamilton's personality were apparently such that it was difficult even for his contemporaries to make sense of him, but the challenges for us are still greater.

Greater but not impossible. Given the span of more than two centuries, it is unrealistic to expect our understanding of Hamilton to be as complete as it is for close contemporaries; but as attested by accomplished biographies and even a musical show, it is possible to get a reasonably filled-in sense of how the political and social issues of the day looked to him and a sense as well of how his sometimes seemingly puzzling behavior fits within an overall story about his life, personality, and times.[26]

---

26. See Ron Chernow, *Alexander Hamilton* (New York: Penguin Books, 2004); Joseph Ellis, *Founding Brothers: The Revolutionary Generation* (New York: Random House, 2000);

But as centuries pass and the circumstances of Hamilton's life come to seem even more foreign to inquirers and their audiences, understanding will become all the more difficult. Imagine a future human society as different from our own as ours is from the Viking culture of the ninth to eleventh centuries. Then picture the inhabitants of this future society trying to come to grips with Hamilton. Talented enough biographers of that society may still be able to weave Hamilton's actions and beliefs into a story that would help their compatriots have some degree of understanding of what to them is an unfamiliar life and time, but their task will be more demanding than the one facing contemporary biographers.

It will be more demanding because, in the search to interpret others, there needs to be a critical mass of similarities between inquirers and those they are trying to understand, which can then be the basis for extrapolations from their own case. Otherwise, there won't be enough material to get the interpretative process started.[27] It is not all or nothing, of course, but as a general rule, the fewer the similarities there are between those who are our subjects and ourselves, the fewer bases we have for using detailed distinctions we can draw from own case to infer correspondingly detailed distinctions about them. Hence, the challenges and limitations we encounter when trying to understand the lives of bats or, for that matter, eleventh-century Vikings.

The situation is inverted when there are extensive similarities between our subjects and ourselves. We are then in a better position to use fine distinctions we have firsthand knowledge of to make

Broadus Mitchell, *Alexander Hamilton: Youth to Maturity 1755–1788,* and *Alexander Hamilton: National Adventure 1788–1804* (New York: Macmillan, 1957 and 1962). The musical is *Hamilton,* lyrics and music by Lin-Manuel Miranda, and based on Chernow's book.

27. See Donald Davidson, "A Coherence Theory of Truth and Knowledge," in *The Philosophy of Donald Davidson,* ed. E. LePore, 307–319 (London: Basil Blackwell, 1986).

comparably fine-grained observations about how our subjects experience the world. It is a curious truth that it is about those who are most like us that we are able to make the most delicately honed distinctions. A Jane Austen or a Henry James is able to turn this into great literature, but there are also chilling possibilities, as when mountains are made out of the molehills of tiny differences to stoke a political agenda against a defined other.

The main lesson for purposes here, however, is that although it is always difficult to understand the richness and complexity of consciousness-related phenomena, when there is such understanding to be had, the humanities along with the arts can help provide it. For a full understanding of many of the issues that arise out of mentality, it is necessary to make use of information that itself displays mentality, as opposed to trying to escape to the extent possible the realm of the mental, as the basic sciences tend to do.

The humanities are thus allied with insights that the sciences in general are not in a good position to capture. That which escapes the sciences lies at the heart of the humanities, but the reverse is also true. The sciences provide insights that cannot be delivered by the humanities. All of this confirms what perhaps should have been obvious from the start—namely, the two are not rivals. They are complementary, with each addressing that which the other is not well equipped to address.

Chapter 4

Related Topics

PHILOSOPHY, THE HUMANITIES, THE SCIENCES

Some of philosophy's fields—metaphysics and philosophy of physics are two examples—are not concerned in significant ways with human societies. For this reason, philosophy is occasionally viewed as not being part of the humanities at all;[1] but in whatever way it is classified, many of its fields do seem more closely aligned with the sciences than with the humanities. Logic has close ties to mathematics, while philosophy of physics, philosophy of mind, philosophy of biology, and philosophy of language address questions associated with their neighboring sciences.

The affinities with science go beyond shared subject matters, however. In all of philosophy's fields, there is a science-like value placed on simplicity and generality. Indeed, it is precisely this preference that Wittgenstein in his late period regarded as responsible for the failings of philosophy as a discipline.

---

1. See Colin McGinn, "Philosophy by Another Name," *New York Times*, March 4, 2012. https://opinionator.blogs.nytimes.com/2012/03/04/philosophy-by-another-name/

I will return to Wittgenstein in a moment, but first, as two case studies, consider logic and ethics. Logic is concerned with principles of correct reasoning, the most elementary of which are rules of deductive logic such as simplification (if $[p$ and $q]$ is true, then p is true); addition (if p is true, then $[p$ or $q]$) is true; noncontradiction (p and *not-p* cannot both be true); and excluded middle (either p or *not-p* is true).

These rules have characteristics that are highly prized in the sciences. They are non-indexical (applying to all subject matters at all times and places) and non-perspectival (not being conditional on the point of view of the inquirer). There is also wide consensus about them. Occasionally there have been disputes about one or another, but in general there is agreement about their acceptability. In addition, they are descriptive, not because they depict how people in fact always reason but because they describe what it is to reason correctly, where this is a matter of moving from truths to other truths. Insofar as the preservation of truth ought to be one's goal in reasoning, one should follow these rules, but logic itself does not dictate this. Its job is to articulate the rules of truth-preserving reasoning.[2]

By contrast, the various ethical theories proposed in the history of philosophy have all been highly contested. This is so even for meta-ethical theories, which are not in the business of making positive ethical recommendations. They restrict themselves to clarifying the general nature of ethical claims and explaining how it is they differ from other claims. But other ethical theories are explicitly prescriptive; they make recommendations about how humans ought to

---

2. See Gilbert Harman, *Change in View* (Cambridge, MA: MIT Press, 1986). For a different view, see Hartry Field, "What Is the Normative Role of Logic?" *Proceedings of the Aristotelian Society* 83 (Suppl., 2009), 251–268.

behave. So, their aim is quite different from the descriptive aim of the sciences, but even this area of ethics shares with the sciences an aspiration for simplicity and generality.

Kant's ethics is a famous example. His aim was to formulate a first principle of ethics that would be adequate for governing the decision making of all rational agents, by which he meant all creatures with a faculty of reason, regardless of when and where they live and what their cultural circumstances might be. As such, it would govern even the decisions of rational creatures whose other faculties might be quite unlike humans and who live in circumstances quite different from humans, if there be such creatures. The principle Kant defended was a "categorical imperative" that requires everyone act in accordance with maxims that can be universal laws.

The utilitarian philosophers such as Bentham and Mill had only slightly less ambitious objectives. They, too, sought to articulate a fundamental principle of ethics with extremely wide scope. Their proposed principle was to maximize the overall balance of pleasures over pains, and they maintained that it should govern every decision, regardless of time, place, and circumstances, with the capacity to affect the prospects of pleasure or pain of sentient creatures.

Neither Kant's categorical imperative nor utilitarianism nor any of the other first principles proposed over the long history of philosophical ethics have generated anything remotely like consensus, but even if agreement on a first principle had somehow been achieved, there would remain the limitation alluded to earlier. If one tries to derive specific recommendations about what to do in concrete situations from a preferred first principle, one is immediately confronted with the immense gap between the generality of the principle and the specificity of the situations in which decisions have to be made. If the principle is to be at all plausible, it must be of an extremely general form, such as "maximize utility" or "act in accordance with maxims that can be universal laws." But principles of this generality are not capable of generating definitive solutions to concrete predicaments.

As mentioned earlier, Sartre tried to use this limitation in his critique of objective values in general. But whatever one's views are about the nature of values, it is not realistic to expect philosophy to generate rules that can be used in a mechanical fashion to sort out all the intricacies of human life. This is not to deny that concrete advice is possible. It is just to admit that philosophical ethics cannot on its own supply it. Advice also has to be grounded in detailed information about the specific situation and its historical and social context.[3]

I will return in a moment to this point, but notice first that the need for contextual grounding here is symptomatic of the involvement that the humanities in general have with indexical considerations. Wherever there is theorizing, there is going to be interest in arriving at conclusions that are general and simple. It is no different in any of the fields of the humanities, but given the nature of their issues and the desire for insights applicable to human lives and societies, there are also countervailing forces pulling one back from the general and simple and toward information about specific individuals, groups, events, and other particularities of time and place. A pullback to indexicality and complexity, in other words.

Because its initial preferences for generality and simplicity are so strong, these pushes and pulls can be especially potent in philosophy. This is most apparent in ethics and other prescriptive fields, such as political philosophy and aesthetics, but it is present to some

---

3. See Bernard Williams, *Ethics and Limits of Philosophy* (London: Routledge, 2006); and Alasdair MacIntyre, *After Virtue: A Study in Moral Theory*, 2nd ed. (Notre Dame, IN: University of Notre Dame Press, 1984).

degree or another in all fields of philosophy, if for no other reason than part of the project is always to clarify and refine key concepts. In ethics, political philosophy, and aesthetics, the concepts are ones such as goodness, justice, beauty, fairness, freedom, and moral responsibility, whereas in the fields of epistemology, metaphysics, philosophy of mind, and philosophy of sciences, they are ones such as truth, rationality, justification, knowledge, time, explanation, time, space, and necessity.

Philosophers have had their differences about how best to go about explicating such concepts, but whatever the approach, efforts of this sort have an indexical cast to them. The aim is to get clear about the commitments and applicability conditions of concepts that have a history and hence are rooted in particularities of time and place. These particularities, in turn, are the source of the problem that so bothered Wittgenstein. His worry was that the value philosophy places on simple, general principles results in distortions at best and paradoxes at worst. This is so because our concepts evolved in specific contexts for specific purposes. As a result, they are complex, variable, and sometimes even in tension with one another, and it is a misplaced impulse to try to simplify them. Doing so invites error.

Wittgenstein further maintained that this misdirected impulse has its source in the view that philosophy is an extension of science. His proposed "therapy" was to give up on positive agendas in philosophy. Its sole function ought to be the therapeutic one of protecting ourselves from an unhealthy yearning for simplicity—this longing for the smooth, flat, and undifferentiated. "Back to the rough ground" was his aphorism. Here is a characteristically blunt passage from his *Blue Book*:

> Our craving for generality has [as one] source ... our preoccupation with the method of science. I mean the method of reducing

the explanation of natural phenomena to the smallest possible number of primitive natural laws; and, in mathematics, of unifying the treatment of different topics by using a generalization. Philosophers constantly see the method of science before their eyes, and are irresistibly tempted to ask and answer in the way science does. This tendency is the real source of metaphysics, and leads the philosopher into complete darkness.[4]

It is possible, however, to have sympathy with the diagnosis that philosophy often places too great a premium on simplicity and uniformity, without committing oneself to the militancy of Wittgenstein's proposed therapy. There is a middle ground, one that is accepting of philosophy's limitations without giving up altogether on the search for general principles. In ethics, the middle ground was anticipated by Aristotle with his commonsense warning not to expect specificity in ethics. He thought that the task of philosophical ethics is to articulate and defend a broad view about what a good human life is, but it need not, and indeed could not, generate definitive resolutions to life's concrete problems. There are similar middle grounds in political philosophy and aesthetics; and for the projects of concept clarification found in all areas of philosophy, the middle ground takes the form of recognizing that while improvements and clarifications of everyday concepts are certainly possible, there should not be an expectation that further refinements and revisions won't be needed as time passes and new circumstances emerge. Nor should there be an expectation that the improvements, real as they

4. Ludwig Wittgenstein, *The Blue and Brown Books* (London: Blackwell, 1958). See also Horwich's treatment of these issues in Paul Horwich, *Wittgenstein's Metaphilosophy* (Oxford: Oxford University Press, 2012).

may be, will result in consensus about philosophy's most contested issues.

This last point is especially important. As extensive as the connections are between philosophy and the sciences, the open-ended character of philosophy's core questions and the absence of realistic prospects for achieving consensus on them over time remains a deep-seated difference. It is the lens through which all other comparisons and contrasts with the sciences need to be seen.

As an illustration, return to the wide gap between the generality of proposed first principles of ethics and the specific contexts in which decisions have to be made. If a first principle is to be at all helpful in the making of these decisions, it has to be supplemented with detailed contextual information. But this may not seem all that different from what occurs in the sciences. Recall geology. Its insights about large-scale motions on the surface of a planet are derived from a set of standing conditions (ones about the different layers of the planet and their distinct properties) and a set of universal or nearly universal forces operating on them (heat conduction, heat convection, friction, gravitation, etc.). Thus, just as proposed first principles of ethics are not on their own capable of generating conclusions about what to do in concrete situations, so too these fundamental physical forces are not on their own able to explain specific events in the geological history of Earth. They do so only when supplemented by extensive information about the context— in this case, the standing environmental conditions that these forces were acting upon.

There is something to this analogy. On the one hand, it illustrates how in both philosophy and the sciences, the very general and the very local can comfortably co-exist. On the other hand, the analogy cannot be pressed too far. For however much information about the context is supplied, with ethical issues there is no realistic hope for arriving at definitive solutions on which there is a consensus. This may be because of the nonobjective nature of values or because in any complex situation multiple values are relevant with no recipe for balancing them. But whatever the explanation, there is not the possibility for the kind of closure on ethical issues that the theory of plate tectonics potentially provides for its issues.

So, although philosophy, like the sciences, tends to place a premium on simple and general insights, the open-ended character of its core issues, and its lack of prospects for achieving consensus on them even over time, is a major difference. This in turn is linked with the further distinction that in philosophy, as in the humanities in general, individual insight is highly valued for its own sake. It is a personal puzzlement, after all, that got many philosophers interested in the field to begin with. Part of what has attracted students to the field since its earliest days is its character as a personal intellectual search. The philosopher's task is to arrive at judgments about the issues that can be accepted in a personal way, not simply to advance a common agenda.[5] A companion observation, made by Richard Fumerton, is that most positions in philosophy are minority positions.[6] So, the attitude to adopt is: "Although I would like others to agree with me, what is critical is arriving at answers to the questions that I am willing to stand behind."

As noted earlier, many scientists are also motivated by personal curiosity, but their investigations take place within a practice that has the expansion of collective knowledge as a central goal. Science is organized to move in the direction of consensus on its issues, whereas this is not feasible for philosophy's core issues.

---

5. Philip Pettit emphasized this point in a Fall 2011 talk at Harvard University.
6. Richard Fumerton, *Knowledge, Thought, and the Case for Dualism* (Cambridge: Cambridge University Press, 2015), 91.

However, this does not mean that philosophy is not a communal enterprise in all the ways the rest of the humanities are, as discussed in chapter 2, the section "Individual vs. Collective." Moreover, those fields of philosophy that are closely associated with particular sciences are communal in additional ways. Philosophers of physics, biology, language, psychology, neuroscience, and so on adopt problems from their sciences; they make use of empirical findings established by the researchers in their sciences; and they make proposals for improving the theories within their sciences. Indeed, so great are these overlaps that it may not seem much of a stretch to view these fields of philosophy as being a part of their affiliated science, and hence also part of that science's collective efforts.[7]

In any event, however extensive the communal elements may be in some of philosophy's fields, they are present to at least some degree in all of its fields. So, none of its inquiries is so individualistic that it should be conducted privately. When done well, the conclusions reached and the arguments mounted in their defense will be of interest to many and persuasive to some; sometimes, as when philosophers take on issues in the sciences or social sciences, they can be of interest to entire disciplines. Besides, conducting the inquiry publicly decreases the chances of being trapped in a bubble of self-reinforcing views, and thus increases the chances of making improvements. Still, in the end, with respect to its central problems, the aim is to arrive at conclusions that one is willing to stand behind even if others disagree.

So, to repeat, although many of philosophy's fields have close ties with the sciences, and although all its fields have a science-like attraction for simple and general principles, it also has features that

---

7. I owe this point to Paul Horwich.

draw it back toward the humanities: the open-ended character of its core issues, which means there is no prospect of an end to inquiry into them; the search for individual insight without the expectation or need for consensus; and the need to introduce contextual complexities if the insights are to have relevance for human lives, societies, and projects.

Fellow guests at a party have sometimes asked me, "How interesting it is that you are a philosopher, but tell me, what's your philosophy?" I usually respond with something earnest and I hope understandable about the field, but occasionally, out of tiredness or perhaps childishness, I have heard myself saying, "Well, my philosophy is quite simple; it's that everything is really more complex than it seems." This has occasionally elicited a response of the form, "I'm so glad to hear you say that; it's just what I think, too." I smile politely and take satisfaction in my private joke—only, as with many jokes, it is not entirely a joke.

STORIES AS SOURCES OF INSIGHT

We tell stories about pretty much everybody and everything. Ourselves, our children, our friends, fellow workers, and pets. Also about countries, ideas, and social practices. Even inanimate objects: houses, cars, and watches.

It is not surprising, then, that scientific insights are also often related in story form. This is especially common in evolutionary biology, where there are narratives about the emergence of different beak sizes and shapes in Galápagos finches, how there came to be peppered moths during the Industrial Revolution, and the origins of modern humans. It is not just biology, however. Cosmology has a story to tell about the early history of the universe and the subsequent formation of galaxies; and geology's story is one about Earth and changes in its surface features.

Although they are employed everywhere as aids to understanding, it is with portrayals of human lives that stories, fictional and factual, find their most refined uses. Both kinds of stories produce insights, although it bears repeating that fictional works, like the rest of the arts, should not be evaluated solely in terms of the knowledge they produce, as if they were mere helpmates of history, sociology, psychology, or philosophy. Still, they are capable of generating insights, not just about the fictional world of the work but also about the real world.

But the latter may seem puzzling. Factual stories are lived before they are told. So, there is nothing especially mystifying about how they convey real-world information—but how is this possible when the stories are about imaginary characters and events? Part of the answer is that they are not entirely imaginative; indeed, they cannot be.

In chapter 2, I discussed how the sciences make extensive use of generalizations about the behavior of phenomena under conditions that rarely if ever obtain, the ideal gas law being an example. The generalizations are nevertheless intended to facilitate predictions and explanations of phenomena in real situations, but there are, as a result, constraints on how idealized the conditions can be. They cannot be so far removed from conditions in the real world as to make the generalizations useless in understanding and accurately predicting actual phenomena. An analogous point applies to fiction. Even highly experimental works cannot depart so drastically from reality that there are no recognizable parallels for audiences to grab onto. There are limits to how completely works of fiction can escape from real-world conditions if they are to be comprehensible, much less be of any use in understanding the actual world.

Most works of fiction do not offer anything like a complete escape, of course. Their departures from reality often occur against a backdrop of extensive information about actual times, places, and events. Dickens created irresistible fictional characters and narratives involving them, but his novels also contain a wealth of information about the details of life in nineteenth-century London, from its legal practices to its debtor prisons. Similarly, Lampedusa's *The Leopard* is the moving personal story of a Sicilian nobleman living out the end of his life during the *Risorgimento,* but it is also an astute guide to the political and social factors underlying the movement to unify Italy. So it is with countless other works of fiction.

These real-world aspects of fiction are allied with what Henry James called its ability to provide an "extension of life." Stories provide audiences with access to people, places, times, and situations with which they have no direct experience. As such, they are potentially powerful instruments for cross-cultural understanding, a point that Anthony Appiah has especially emphasized. He observes that people everywhere have an ability to follow a narrative and, indeed, seem positively eager to hear stories even about that which is foreign to them. These stories have the capacity to illustrate in concrete ways how behavior, traditions, and practices that initially look bewildering or perhaps even perverse might nonetheless fit within another way of thinking or living. The insights, however, are not dependent on the stories being able to generate a consensus on high-level moral, political, or social principles. The points of agreement and mutual understanding can be much more local. One of Appiah's examples is that individuals in very different circumstances do not necessarily need robust theoretical arguments to arrive at agreement on the need for helping a particular child in a specific difficult situation. Telling the child's story is often enough.[8] Even a photo that is suggestive of a story can be enough, as was the case with the photo of a bewildered five-year-old Syrian boy coated with dust and blood after an airstrike on Aleppo.[9] Fiction's ability to inform and instruct can work similarly. By embedding characters in richly described contexts, skillful narratives help audiences understand and have sympathy with ways of acting and thinking far removed from their own.

There are complementary hypotheses about the social and political importance of such stories. One class of arguments begins by noting the enormous increase in literacy over the last several centuries, which, when combined with advances in publication and media technologies, has provided wide swaths of people with increased access to stories, both fictional and nonfictional, about those who are different from them. The hypothesis is that these stories, with their depictions of the variety of human lives and the distinct points of view associated with them, have enhanced appreciation of and tolerance for diverse ways of living, which in turn has helped to create a climate where stronger commitments to human rights become, if not inevitable, at least more feasible.[10]

The power of fiction to inform and instruct is not limited to the distant, however. There are also insights to be had close to home, even ones about that which is most familiar. This again may seem

---

8. Kwame Anthony Appiah, *The Ethics of Identity* (Princeton, NJ: Princeton University Press, 2005).

9. "How Omran Daqneesh, 5, Became a Symbol of Aleppo's Suffering," *New York Times*, August 18, 2016. https://www.nytimes.com/2016/08/19/world/middleeast/omran-daqneesh-syria-aleppo.html

10. See Lynn Hunt, *The Invention of Human Rights: A History* (New York: W.W. Norton, 2007); Steven Pinker, *The Better Angels in Our Nature: Why Violence Has Declined* (New York: Viking-Penguin, 2011); and Elaine Scarry, "Poetry, Injury, and the Ethics of Reading," in *The Humanities and the Public Life*, ed. P. Brooks (New York: Fordham University Press, 2014), 41–48.

a little puzzling, or at least more so than insights about people and events distant in time, place, or culture. How can stories about unreal characters and situations help audiences better understand the real people and situations that they regularly observe firsthand?

Take a step back. Although fiction is not history, there are parallels between the writing of the one and the writing of the other. Just as historians can look widely or narrowly in search of historical understanding, focusing either on detailed events, people, and actions or on larger political or economic forces, fiction writers have analogous choices to make about the scope of their narratives. And even once the scope is settled, they have to decide which of a potentially limitless set of details about characters and settings to omit and which to include, what emphases to put on those that are included, what order to present them, and so on.

These storytelling decisions determine the particularities of the narrative and influence the reader's understanding of how and why the fictional events unfold as they do. They draw attention to features of the characters or situations that are important difference makers in the fictional world of the work, but these features can also be difference makers in the real world—and not just distant situations but also nearby ones. By highlighting in the fictional universe aspects that we tend to overlook or not sufficiently appreciate in our actual environments, fiction can reveal surprising aspects even about what we think we know best. Once again this brings to mind history, where insights about situations and people in one context can reveal structures, patterns, and tendencies that may be helpful for understanding elsewhere. In the same way and for the same reason, insights about fictional events and people can be helpful in understanding real-life counterparts. Indeed, "helpful" understates the case. At its best, fiction has the capacity to fundamentally reorient what one regards as important in thinking about the individuals, events, and practices that surround one.

The dual capacity of stories to help us get a better handle on both the faraway and nearby is in large part the result of their being such effective means for understanding human points of views. They draw readers imaginatively into the worlds of the characters and display how the events being related looked to them, and how this in turn affected their reactions. But of course, the points of view of the storytellers themselves, not just their characters, also matter. Stories are told by authors who have their own peculiar perspectives and for audiences who likewise have distinctive perspectives. So, like the accounts of consciousness-suffused issues in the humanities, stories are triply tinged with perspective: those of the people, societies, or times being narrated, those of the intended audience, and those of the author. Each corner of this triangle is linked with the others. There are author–story links, story–reader links, and author–reader links. For readers, the initial focus is often on the story, its characters, and its events; but the sense of encounter with the mind of the author can be as gripping as the unfolding of events being narrated. Intimacy with others is something almost all of us crave, and the reading of a skillfully crafted story can be just that: an act of intimacy.[11]

There is much more to be said, and has been said, about all these points, but underlying all the questions and theories about how narratives, including fictional ones, can be sources of understanding is the fact of their ubiquity. Why is this? Why is it that stories about human lives, fiction and factual, seem to be found wherever there are human societies? And why do they have such a strong appeal?

11. See Terence Cave, *Thinking with Literature: Towards a Cognitive Criticism* (Oxford: Oxford University Press, 2016).

One explanation is that they are indispensable. They are not merely convenient and entertaining options; they are essential for understanding. We need them in order to make sense of ourselves to ourselves. Self-understanding requires that we put the events of our lives into some kind of narrative form, and the same is true of efforts to understand those around us. We need narratives about them as well.

One of the foremost proponents of this view is Alasdair MacIntyre, who has argued that it is not possible to have the kind of understanding we want of human behavior outside of narrative frameworks. In its sketchiest form, his argument is that we cannot understand human action independently of the agent's intention, but in turn we cannot understand intentions independently of the agent's context and long-term goals. Moreover, for MacIntyre, who was strongly influenced by Aristotle, the most fundamental long-term goal of humans is to have a richly satisfying, purposeful life. This is what all, or virtually all, humans most deeply want, even if they are often confused about how to go about leading such a life. This goal, in turn, imposes a structure on human lives. They have a determinate arc—a beginning, a middle, and an end that together constitute the beginnings of a story about how good the life was. So, it was not just a happy historical accident that ancient poems and sagas told stories about what happened to individual humans. From the very beginning, stories aimed at capturing a narrative structure that human lives inevitably have, and it is this that explains why we are storytelling animals. We make sense of ourselves through the stories in which we are a part and around which we organize our various identities. The same is true for our efforts to understand others; and going up a level in generality, it is even true for societies as a whole. The best way to arrive at an overall understanding of a society, whether our own or another, is through its collective stock of stories.[12]

As different a philosopher as Sartre agrees that humans have an almost irresistible tendency to be storytellers, but he has a more acerbic take on why. On the one hand, he famously maintained that there is no set human nature and that as a result we humans are radically free to make what we will of ourselves. On the other hand, he also argued that we find this degree of freedom and the responsibility that goes with it so frightening that we are disposed, both individually in our everyday lives and collectively in our social practices, to find ways to pretend we are less free than we actually are. The stories we tell about ourselves and others are a part of this flight from freedom.

So, contrary to what MacIntyre claims, Sartre's view is that storytelling is not to be understood as an effort to reveal the preexisting structures of human lives. Quite the opposite. Stories are after-the-fact attempts to impose order. Like MacIntyre, Sartre sees stories as ways to express identities—our own or those of others. They are meant to illustrate what kind of people we (or they) are: courageous, introverted, adventurous, loyal, friendly, honest, jealous, or whatever. But these identities, says Sartre, are always falsifying, since they never fully capture who we are. We could have chosen, and still can choose, to be different, and it is "bad faith" to think otherwise. But if these identities are falsifying, so too are the stories that give expression to them.[13]

Once again, there is more to be debated, and worth debating, about these arguments, but for purposes here, what is most important

---

12. MacIntyre, *After Virtue: A Study in Moral Theory.* For related views, see Appiah, *The Ethics of Identity;* and Charles Taylor, *The Ethics of Authenticity* (Cambridge: Cambridge University Press, 1991).
13. Sartre, *Existentialism is a Humanism.* (New Haven, CT: Yale University Press, 2007).

are fiction's conspicuous analogies with the humanities. Works of fiction are not to be evaluated solely in terms of whether they produce insights, but when they do, the insights have the same central features as those in the humanities. They are almost always highly indexical; they often have prescriptive elements; they are triply tinged with perspective; and there is a premium on individual insight.

Works of fiction likewise share the secondary features characteristic of the humanities: there is deep involvement with issues of mentality; the target audience is limited; there tends to be a built-in appreciation of complexity and a wariness of simplicity; the manner of influence on the opinions of the audience is principally Socratic; there is no natural stopping point in efforts to interpret them; and likewise, no matter how successful they may be, there need be no end to attempts to develop even more incisive fictional treatments of the topics and themes they address.

The humanities and the sciences, as I have said, are not rivals, but the humanities and the arts are family.

A QUICK LOOK AT THE SOCIAL SCIENCES

I have largely bypassed the social sciences, the presupposition being that they occupy a midpoint between the natural sciences and the humanities. Like the natural sciences, they strive to be descriptive. They also tend to place a high value on collective knowledge. But because they deal with human societies, there are sharper constraints than in the natural sciences on efforts to minimize indexicality. And because many issues about human societies cannot be fully addressed without understanding the points of views of the individuals making up the societies, there are also greater challenges in minimizing perspectivality.

These are only rough generalizations, however. When one looks at the social sciences, one sees great diversity. Even within particular disciplines, there is variety, with some subfields leaning toward the natural sciences and others much less so. In anthropology, physical anthropology makes extensive use of methods it shares with the natural sciences, but cultural anthropology does not. Other social science disciplines are similarly divisible.

The science-leaning wings of social science disciplines make extensive use of mathematics, statistics, and formal modeling techniques, and many of the important findings of the last century in the social sciences have come out of such work. One prominent example is Kenneth Arrow's impossibility theorem, which challenges the cherished assumption of democracies that voting turns individual preferences into collective preferences that express the general will. Arrow proved that there are conditions, and not especially unusual ones, in which it is not possible for voting to generate outcomes that satisfy certain natural constraints, such as transitivity: if A is preferred to B and B is preferred to C, A is preferred to C.[14]

The power of Arrow's theorem comes at least in part from its being derived from formal techniques that, as in the natural sciences, reduce the influence of perspectival and indexical factors. Other subfields in the social sciences, by contrast, deliberately emphasize perspectival and indexical factors, as opposed to trying to minimize them. Ethnographic methods, which were pioneered and refined in anthropology but are now effectively used across a range of social science disciplines, are a case in point. Investigators personally immerse themselves in the society under study, make extensive firsthand observations of the people in their own environments, and then often supplement these observations with personal

14. Kenneth Arrow, *Social Choice and Individual Values* (New York: John Wiley, 1951).

interviews, all of which are intended to provide them with a sense of how the society looks from the points of view of its own members.

Even in subfields that traditionally employ such methods, however, there sometimes are movements aimed at reducing indexicality and encouraging the development of hypotheses that are general and simple—in other words, hypotheses that have features characteristic of the basic sciences. That there are such movements should not be surprising. There is no single best way of understanding human lives, societies, and histories. In the search for understanding, one can always look more widely or more narrowly. So, wherever there is theorizing, there are going to be those whose tendency it is to push for greater generality and simplicity.

I earlier discussed how this tendency affects philosophy, but one also sees it across the social sciences. But because they are investigating human societies, there inevitably also are forces pulling inquiries back in the direction of specificity and complexity. Thus, cultural anthropology has witnessed not only the rise of structuralism, which seeks to uncover general patterns in the practices and activities of all human cultures,[15] but also counter movements that encourage inquirers to develop "thick" descriptions of cultural practices, the presupposition being that cultures tend to display the same kinds of internal complexity, diversity, and conflicting impulses one finds in individual people.[16]

Here's a story I like to keep in mind when thinking about such issues. Levittown, New York, was the first mass-produced suburb in the United States. The ranch homes making up Levittown came in five models, but the models were virtually identical in layout and

---

15. Claude Levi-Strauss, *The Savage Mind* (Chicago: University of Chicago Press, 1966).
16. Clifford Geertz, "Thick Description: Toward an Interpretive Theory of Culture," in *The Interpretation of Cultures: Selected Essays* (New York: Basic Books, 1973), 3–30.

design, the only differences being ones of exterior color and window placements. In 2000, for the fiftieth anniversary of its founding, filmmakers set out to make a documentary about Levittown and its place in American culture, but when they visited the site to film what the original houses looked like, they had trouble finding ones that had not been substantially altered by their owners over the years. Some now had garages whereas none of the originals did; others had porches; yet others had fenced yards; some had second floor dormers; and so on.

My optimistic takeaway from this little story, although I admit the optimism may be as much an act of will as a finding, is that even in the face of pressures for uniformity, individuality finds a way to break out. There is a corresponding intellectual lesson, however— one that is less clouded by wishful thinking and, rather, echoes a familiar refrain of this essay. Namely, when trying to understand phenomena associated with consciousness, the search should not be restricted to insights of great generality and simplicity. Creatures exhibiting mentality create phenomena of nuance and diversity, and a taste for only the simple and general risks glossing over much that is of interest. There ought also to be a taste for complexity.

Chapter 5

Conclusion

A Plea for Intellectual Humility

There is a moral dimension to inquiry, whether it be in the sciences, humanities, or any other field. The responsibility is to conduct inquiries in intellectually virtuous ways. There are many such virtues—disinterestedness, thoroughness, and imaginativeness, to name just a few—but the one that I want to make a special plea for is intellectual humility. The plea, moreover, is not just for an occasional whiff of it but, rather, for a permeating, ever-present humility that constantly cautions against overconfidence. The humility I have in mind is not to be equated with timidity, however. It is compatible with large ambitions and risk-taking, but at the end of the day, after all the work and effort, there should be a recognition of the possibility of having gotten things wrong. It may be the special circumstances one finds oneself in that calls for humility, but there is also a ground for it that arises out of the very nature of inquiry and hence is always and everywhere appropriate. It is appropriate for scholars, for other inquirers, and for everyone else as well. A humility for all and about all.

But let's begin with the more local. Individuals often are not in a good position to form an opinion on an issue. With respect to everyday matters, such as whether it is raining outside or how many people attended an opening, the problem may be that they simply are not (or were not) in the right time and right place to observe the situation firsthand—and neither was anyone else whom they know and trust. With respect to more complex issues, however, including those grappled with by investigators in the sciences and humanities, the problem can be a lack of expertise as well as of information. Nonexperts usually do not have all the relevant information, but they also have not had the training that would allow them to adequately assess the information even if they did have it.

In the book's preface, I commented on the need for universities to have both a long view and a broad view. The same is true of individuals. Some issues are not important enough to demand sustained, serious investigation, but many are. For them, it is a lengthy project to accumulate all the relevant evidence and all the skills necessary to deal with the issues satisfactorily. As a result, it is not possible for anyone, no matter how smart and energetic, to accumulate the breadth of expertise and information that would be needed to reliably form opinions in every field.

Virtually everyone agrees with this sentiment in theory, but in practice humans are inveterate believers. And so they often find it tempting, whether from the press of other business or simple impatience, to form opinions on their own about matters they are not in a good position to judge. If the issue is of minor importance or their view about it is only loosely held, there need be no great harm. But it often seems as if firmness and stubbornness of conviction go up rather than down with the importance of the issue and the narrowness of the information on which the opinion is based.

Perhaps this has always been so,[1] but a declining regard for intellectual humility may also be a side effect of a culture that tends to be

---

1. See John Henry Newman, "Discourse IV," *The Idea of a University* (Notre Dame, IN: Notre Dame Press, 2016).

obsessed with self-expression. Having and stating opinions comes to be seen as a presentation of one's identity, as opposed to a reflection of one's information and training. Opinions, like emotions, are not to be bottled up inside. It can even be seen as a mark of a slippery personality not to have strong views staked out on a wide range of subjects.

So, as obvious as the option of not taking a stand on an issue is in principle, in practice it is often neglected. When pressed for an opinion, "I'm not in a position to judge" may not be a welcomed response, but it is frequently the right one. It is an acknowledgment that one ought to withhold judgment about a topic until one has adequate information and the necessary skills to assess it—or if this is not feasible, until one has the views of those who do have the relevant information and training. For, an aspect of intellectual humility is a corresponding respect for expertise. If one is not well positioned to reach an opinion on one's own, deference to the opinions of those who are well positioned is in order; or if the issue is one that resists outright deference, at least a willingness to be guided by specialists is called for—an openness, that is, to Socratic influence.

But which specialists? If one is not able to assess the truth of claims in a subject area, how can one go about assessing the reliability of supposed specialists? Those who have a stake in politicizing expertise will insist that there is no satisfactory answer to this question, but this is overly pessimistic. There are times when identifying a relevant expert is an intractable problem, but as a rule people can find ways to make the needed assessments. Often it is by means of second-level trust. People rely on experts they know and trust in one field for advice about experts in neighboring fields, as when one turns to one's internist for guidance on cardiologists. Comparisons of the credentials and amounts of experience of specialists can also be helpful. In addition, there are sometimes public rankings and online assessments of various sorts to consult, and of course there are always trusted family members, friends, and colleagues who may be able to provide relevant information. The bottom line is that if one is willing to make the effort, it is usually possible to locate someone (or some group) for informed advice about which experts to trust.[2]

Then again, to state another commonplace, expert opinion is not always correct opinion. Experts have training and access to information that others lack, but this does not mean they don't make mistakes and don't have all the usual human frailties. They are sometimes sloppy, inattentive, forgetful, or ideological. The list of their potential failings is as long as that of humans generally. So, even after one has reasonably reached a conclusion about which experts are most trustworthy, there remain questions about the limits of the trust one should place in them.

By the same token, these are also questions for the experts to ask of themselves. They, too, need to be cognizant of their limits. All else being equal, they are expected not to straddle the fence on issues in their fields. If they lack relevant information or training, their default responsibility is to try to get it. At times however, this may not be easy or even possible. The evidence may point in both directions or crucial data may be lacking. So, they, too, need to be on guard against overconfidence. They have to be able to judge when to admit: "I'm not yet in a position to have a view."

And even when they do have access to sufficient evidence, they still need to be disinterested, thorough, and careful in their handling of it and in drawing conclusions from it. These may sound like routine warnings, but recent work in cognitive psychology has revealed

---

2. Tom Nichols, *The Death of Expertise* (New York: Oxford University Press, 2017); and John Hardwig, "Epistemic Dependence," *Journal of Philosophy* 82, no. 7 (July 1985): 335–349.

just how difficult it sometimes can be to heed them. It is difficult because humans have general tendencies, which they often are not aware of, to be unreliable in the ways they process certain kinds of information. It has become a bit of a cottage industry for psychologists to search for these predispositions to error, and they have been successful. There is now a large, somewhat depressing inventory of the kinds of mistakes people regularly make.

Of course, no one should be shocked to learn that we humans are prone to error. When we are tired, emotionally distressed, inebriated, or just too much in a hurry, we tend of make mistakes. The recent findings are disturbing for another reason. They document our susceptibilities to making certain kinds of errors even when we are not disadvantaged in any of the usual ways. We have a tendency to neglect base rates when evaluating statistical claims; we are subject to anchoring effects (an overreliance on early information) when we deliberate about issues; we suffer from overconfidence biases in assessing our own abilities. Short personal interviews with applicants for schools, jobs, parole, and so on regularly worsen rather than improve the accuracy of our predictions about the future performance of candidates. And the list goes on and on.[3]

When learning of such findings, the pressing personal question becomes: How should they affect the confidence one has in one's opinions? The most important thing to say about this question is pretty simple—namely, don't ignore the findings. Moreover, this injunction applies as much to experts as it does to anyone else. It is, after all, part of their professional responsibility as experts to be on

---

3. For some of the pioneering work on these issues, see R. E. Nisbett and L. Ross, *Human Inference: Strategies and Shortcomings of Social Judgement* (Englewood Cliffs, NJ: Prentice-Hall, 1980); and Daniel Kahneman, Paul Slovic, and Amos Tverski, eds., *Judgement under Uncertainty: Heuristics and Biases* (Cambridge: Cambridge University Press, 1982). For an accessible overview of the issues, see Daniel Kahneman, *Thinking, Fast and Slow* (New York: Farrar, Straus and Giroux, 2011).

the lookout for any signs of unreliability. Besides, taking the findings seriously in a personal way is an expression of intellectual humility and the respect for expertise that should accompany it. The relevant respect here is that of experts in one field for those in other fields—in this case, for the cognitive psychologists whose research has surfaced these problems.

Still, one does not have to be paralyzed by the findings. Becoming aware and keeping in mind the predispositions to make mistakes of the documented sort can be helpful in avoiding them. To be forewarned is often enough to be forearmed. This is not always the case, but enough so that one can be entitled to have confidence, even if not certainty, in one's judgments if one has monitored oneself for such problems and done so in intellectually virtuous ways—that is, disinterestedly, thoroughly, and so on.

There is, however, an even more general worry to come to grips with, one not arising from local contexts or the ways humans tend to process information but, rather, from the nature of inquiry itself. As such, it is present no matter how virtuously inquiry is conducted. It derives from there being no foolproof marks for when we have arrived at truths. There are no such guarantees for us individually, however expert we may be, and no guarantees for us collectively. Each person's intellectual history is sprinkled with mistakes, and so is the history of human thought generally. Many of these errors could have been avoided with more care, but it is a sobering reality that no matter how meticulously we have conducted our inquiries, there are no completely airtight assurances that we have gotten things right.

To many, this may seem a humdrum observation, but there are those who have resisted it, and they are not just the doctrinaire or naive. No less an intellect than Descartes found it intolerable that he as an individual and humans in general were vulnerable to mistakes.

He sought a method for avoiding error and thought he had found it. He maintained that one could be assured of not falling into error provided one's standards were sufficiently strict, and he had a specific recommendation about what was strict enough. One should assent only to claims whose truth on reflection is utterly impossible to doubt.

There are questions that Descartes tried to answer about what kinds of claims can meet this demanding criterion, but in anticipation of objections, he also raised a deeper theoretical question about his recommendation. Might not we be psychologically constituted such that even some of the things we find impossible to doubt are nonetheless false? His answer was that God would not permit this, but once again, anticipating objections, he recognized that this merely pushes back the questions to ones about the existence and purposes of God. To deal with these, Descartes daringly mounted what he claimed were a pair of indubitable arguments to establish that, first, God exists and, second, being all good and all powerful, God would not permit us to be deceived about that which is indubitable for us.

Not many have agreed that his arguments, for these conclusions are in fact impossible to doubt; but a more awkward problem is that even if they had been indubitable, this still would not have been enough to provide absolute guarantees of truth. If the worry one is trying to address is that indubitable claims might nonetheless be false, it does not help to invoke indubitable considerations in the refutation. This is the notorious problem of the Cartesian circle noted by many commentators.

What is less frequently appreciated is that Descartes's problem is also ours. We may not be as fixated as he was on eliminating any and all chance of error, but we, too, would like to be assured that our core faculties and methods are at least generally reliable.

If, however, we use these same methods and faculties in trying to provide the assurances, we will not have secured the guarantees we seek, whereas if we try to rely on other methods and faculties in the defense, we can then ask about their reliability, and all the same problems arise again. This is a generalization of the problem of the Cartesian circle, and it is one from which we can no more escape than could Descartes.

One possible reaction is despair—to throw up one's hands and declare there is no point to inquiry; one set of opinions about the world is as good as any other. A more mature response is to live with uncertainty, acknowledging that the lack of guarantees is part of the human intellectual condition. We all are working intellectually without a safety net, but that is no reason to give up. There are still inquiries worth pursuing, they can still be conducted in better or worse ways, and the results can still be more or less compelling. What is required, however, is that all inquiry, whether in the sciences or the humanities or anywhere else, be undertaken in a spirit of intellectual humility—one that accepts that there are no infallible marks of truth or reliability.

Keeping this lesson in mind is an antidote to dogmatism. Those who wrap themselves in certitude find it easy to dismiss anyone or anything that might unsettle their favored opinions. Negative evidence is discounted, new methods not taken seriously, and the arguments for long-held views rarely reexamined. Intellectual humility as a core value encourages just the opposite: an openness to new evidence, methods, and arguments.

Humility and openness are appropriate attitudes even for those who have immense expertise in their fields. All the more so, they are the attitudes that those lacking expertise in a field ought to have toward the findings of those who do have such expertise. And since no one has expertise in all fields, they are also the attitudes that specialists in one field should have when considering issues in fields where they lack expertise. In particular, they are the attitudes those in the humanities ought to have toward work in the sciences, and those in the sciences have toward work in the humanities.

The central claim of this book has been that the humanities and sciences are different. Their issues are different, their inquiries into their issues are different, and the resulting knowledge is different, but these differences complement one another. That which is at heart of humanities tends to escape the sciences, and vice versa. At the same time, there is no utterly sharp dividing line between the two. The features distinguishing them come in degrees, their home issues touch on one another, and here is where humility again enters: there are no grounds for either to ignore or discount the other. The sciences cannot regard its methods as the suitable ones for everything of interest to us, but for its part, the humanities are not free to take no notice of the findings of the sciences.

INDEX

Sellars, Wilfrid, 18
Shakespeare, William, 14, 65
Shanghai Ranking of Universities, xiii
Shekman, Randy, 76
simplicity, 74–79, 93–102, 112–113
Slovic, Paul, 118
Small, Helen, 55
Snow, C. P., 38
social psychology, 81, 89
social sciences, 5, 89, 110–113
Socratic influence, 42–43, 69–74
Stich, Stephen, 87
stories and storytelling
    as a source of insights, 88–89, 102–110
    universal appeal, 104, 107–109
Street, Sharon, 28
Strevens, Michael, 84

taxonomies, 10
tetrachromatic vision, 86
theism, 24
thick descriptions, 28–29, 112

Timbutku, mosques of, x
trust, intellectual, 67–68
Tverski. Amos, 118

United Arab Emirates, xii
universities
    German model, x
    history and mission, ix–xi
    political and cultural
        challenges, of x
    responsibilities of, x–xi
    in the United Kingdom, xii–xiv
    in the United States, xii–xiv
University of Notre Dame, vii

value judgements. *See* prescriptive claims
value monism, 49
van Fraassen, Bas, 53
viticulture, 11

Williams, Bernard, 16, 28, 96
Wittgenstein, Ludwig, 97–98
women's rights movement, 57